GOOD TIME EATIN' IN CAJUN COUNTRY

Cajun Vegetarian Cooking

by Donna Simón

Book Publishing Company
Summertown, Tennessee

Cover design by Page/Curtis
Interior design by Sheryl Karas
Photos/artwork by Donna Simón, Ellen Isaacs,
              Warren C. Jefferson, and Jerry Lee Hutchens

Printed in the United States by Book Publishing Company
PO Box 99
Summertowm, TN 38483

ISBN 1-57067-005-6

Simón, Donna, 1949-
    Good time eatin' in Cajun country : Cajun vegetarian cooking / by Donna Simón
      p.   cm.
    Includes index.
    ISBN 1-57067-005-6
    1. Vegetarian cookery. 2. Cookery, Cajun. 3. Cookery–Louisiana.
    I. Title.
    TX837.S487 1994
    641.5'636–dc20   94-43213
                                                                              CIP

Calculations for the nutritional analyses in this book are based on the average number of servings listed with the recipes and the average amount of an ingredient if a range is called for. Calculations are rounded up to the nearest gram. If two options for an ingredient are listed, the first one is used. Not included are optional ingredients, serving suggestions, or fat used for frying, unless the amount of fat is specified in the recipe.

Dedicated to MaMa, Mamma, and Flennis.
Flennis, thank you for your patience and support.

Contents

▼▼▼

Introduction   5

Notes From Our Kitchen   6

Breakfast   10

Salads and Salad Dressings   24

Soups and Sandwiches   30

Main Dishes   44

Side Dishes and Sauces   69

Breads   86

Desserts   92

Introduction

▼▼▼

Good Time Eating in Cajun Country came about as a companion book to *Recipes from Our Healthful Kitchen*. I am of Cajun-French descent, and I wanted the recipes that so many people appreciate from that region of Louisiana to be enjoyed by those of us who either no longer eat meat or dairy products and by people who just want to lower their cholesterol and eat a more healthful diet. The flavor has not been forfeited in the transition.

I grew up with a Cajun grandmother and mother, and my husband is also of Cajun descent. In the area we grew up in, great food is a big part of the life-style. After eliminating animals and animal by-products from my diet, I decided to develop recipes for my family and friends that would keep the traditional tastes and style.

Cooking good-tasting food does not have to be complicated or difficult, and it doesn't require meat. It can be simple and easy. It doesn't have to contain cholesterol or be high in fat. All of the following recipes contain no cholesterol and are wonderful. May you enjoy them all.

With love,
Donna Simón

Traditional Cajun cooking calls for a lot of oil. I have modified these recipes to try and preserve the tastes and textures of the original foods, while reducing the amount of fat that is used. In many of the recipes the amount of oil for cooking can be further reduced by using non-stick pans or well-tempered cast iron pans and a little water. Cooking in less oil also requires a little more attention to the cooking process. The food must be stirred more often to avoid sticking. In some cases, reducing the oil may change the texture and richness of the food, but in many dishes there is almost no difference at all. A great deal of the true flavor and aroma of Cajun cooking is conveyed by the spices and combinations of ingredients.

Notes From Our Kitchen

▼▼▼▼▼▼▼▼▼▼▼▼▼▼▼▼▼▼▼▼▼▼▼▼▼▼▼▼▼▼▼▼

Arrowroot Powder: A powdered root that I use in the same way as corn starch.

Baking Powder: Always use baking powder that is aluminum free. There are several on the market. The brand I prefer is Rumford.

Cajun: Cajuns are the descendants of the French who colonized Nova Scotia, which was at one time Acadia. Because of abuse by the British and their land being taken away, they migrated to Southern Louisiana. Here they created a new way of life.

Chick-Pea Flour: Chick-pea flour is ground garbanzo beans. It is very flavorful and it can be found in shops that specialize in foods from India.

Creole: Literally, Creole means a white person of European ancestry. But in Louisiana, Creole can also apply to people of Spanish, French, and African ancestry. One of the most influential people in my life is a Creole French woman whose name is Gladys. Her Creole cooking is the best and very different than my Cajun grandmother. You will find her Creole influence in some of these recipes.

Eggless Mayonnaise: I feel it is important not to use eggs, and most mayonnaise contains eggs. One brand that I like is Nayonaise. It can be found at most health food stores.

Filé (pronounced fee-lay): Filé is a spice used in many Cajun or Creole dishes. It is made from young, dried sassafras leaves. Some brands are a mixture of sassafras and thyme.

Nutritional Yeast: Nutritional yeast (saccharomyces cerevisiae) is a great source of B vitamins and is 40% protein. It has a nutty, cheesy taste and makes a delicious substitute for Parmesan cheese on pastas. Nutritional yeast is not the same as brewer's yeast or other yeasts. It is available in both flake or powder form at most health food stores. It is also sold through Mail Order Catalogs (page 9).

Oil: I always use edible, cold pressed oil. I do not use cottonseed oil because it is heavily sprayed.

Organic: It is becoming more and more urgent to eat organic food. There are a number of pesticides that are used on plants that are very toxic to the human body. Try to find a local farmers market or farmer that you can buy from.

Roux (pronounced rue): This is the basis of Cajun and Creole cooking. Roux is browned flour and oil that is mixed and cooked until the desired color is obtained. It can range from light to almost burnt brown. You can make a low-fat dry roux in pan or in the oven, but dry roux should only be cooked to a light brown.

Soy Cheese: There are several brands of soy cheese on the market today. Some of them are very delicious. I would suggest that you try several different brands. They are a lot like cheese and are used the same way.

Sweeteners: Actually, I should just say honey, because it is the only sweetener I use. It is the least processed of all the sweeteners. I prefer clover honey that is sweet and golden in color but does not have a strong honey taste. Dark honey is bitter and too strong for baking. Some health food stores sell honey in bulk and have great clover honey. You can also try to find a local bee keeper who can supply light clover honey.

Textured Vegetable Protein: This is another great soy product that can be used in place of ground beef. It is very chewy, low in fat, and comes in different sizes. It will take on the flavor of the seasonings you use. Textured vegetable protein can be purchased at most health food stores, or be ordered through Mail Order Catalogs (page 9).

Whole Wheat Pastry Flour: I mention this because I have ruined so many recipes by using regular whole wheat flour. Whole wheat pastry flour is made from a softer wheat berry and makes a finer, lighter flour. I use it exclusively.

Mail Order Companies

▼▼

Tony Chachere's
P. O. Box 1687
Opelousas, LA 70571
800-551-9066
Specializing in Cajun spice mixtures.

K-Pauls
824 Distributors Row
P. O. Box 23342
New Orleans, LA 70183-0342
800-457-2857
Specializing in Cajun spice mixtures
and novelty items. Not particularly
healthy ingredients but a novelty none
the less.

Falcon Trading Co.
1055 17th Ave.
Santa Cruz, CA 95062
800-655-3252
Specializing in organic healthy foods,
juices, and bulk items.

Lhasa Karnak
2513 Shattuck Ave.,
Berkeley, CA 94704
510-548-0380
Specializing in herbs and spices,
ginseng, tea blends, salves, vitamins,
and Homeopathic supplies.

Harvest Direct Inc.
P. O. Box 4514
Decatur, IL 62525
800-835-2867
Specializing in TVP® of different sizes.

Vik Distributors
726 Allston Way
Berkeley, CA 94710
510-644-4412
Fax 510-644-3903
Specializing in chick-pea flour, spices,
and chunk textured vegetable protein.

The Mail Order Catalog
P. O. Box 180 - BC
Summertown, TN 38483
800-695-2241
Specializing in all types of textured vegetable protein,
nutritional yeast, instant gluten flour, low-fat soy powder,
and vegetarian cookbooks.

Breakfast

Southern Homefries

4 medium potatoes,
** diced small**
1 medium onion, minced
¼ cup oil
½ teaspoon salt
cayenne to taste

In a large skillet, fry the potatoes in the oil for 20 minutes flipping a couple of times with a spatula. Add the onion and salt, and cook on medium high heat until everything begins to brown. Give the potatoes a chance to brown a little before flipping again with a spatula. Don't stir too often and the potatoes won't get mushy. It is better to put the cayenne on the potatoes after they have been cooked and served.

Serves 4 to 5

Per serving: Calories: 222, Protein: 2 gm.,
Carbohydrates: 27 gm., Fat: 12 gm.

Homefried Scramble

1 lb tofu, crumbled
½ teaspoon turmeric

Make the Southern Homefries, and add the tofu and turmeric when you add the onions.

Serves 5 to 6

Per serving: Calories: 301, Protein: 13 gm.,
Carbohydrates: 26 gm., Fat: 16 gm.

Biscuits and Cream Gravy

Biscuits:
3 cups whole wheat pastry
   flour
3 teaspoons baking powder
1 teaspoon salt
⅓ cup oil
¾ cup low-fat soymilk
   or water

Preheat the oven to 350°. Mix the dry ingredients together, mix the oil and the soymilk together, and combine the two mixtures. Mix well, even if you have to use your hands. Thorough mixing makes a better biscuit. Roll out 1 inch thick, and cut with a cookie cutter or a glass. Place biscuits on an oiled cookie sheet next to each other, and bake at 350° for 30 minutes or until golden.

Serves 6

Per serving: Calories: 306, Protein: 8 gm., Carbohydrates: 40 gm., Fat: 12 gm.

Variation ☛   Onion Biscuits
Made the same as Biscuits, but add **½ cup onions, chopped and sautéed.**

Cream Gravy:
½ cup whole wheat pastry
   flour
¼ cup oil
1 small onion, thinly sliced
2 cups low-fat soymilk
1½ cups water
1 teaspoon salt
2 teaspoons paprika
⅛ teaspoon cayenne

In a large skillet, lightly brown the flour in the oil, stirring constantly. Immediately add the onion and stir until the onion becomes translucent. Add the remaining ingredients, lower the heat, and cook until the gravy becomes creamy. More water may be added for a thinner gravy. For a richer gravy, use only soymilk for the liquid.

Serves 6

Per serving: Calories: 148, Protein: 3 gm., Carbohydrates: 13 gm., Fat: 9 gm.

Variations ☞ **Brown Gravy**

Made the same as Cream Gravy, but substitute **3 cups of water** for the water and soymilk, and cook the flour until it is a darker brown.

Serves 6

Per serving: Calories: 118, Protein: 1 gm., Carbohydrates: 8 gm., Fat: 9 gm.

☞ **Brown Mushroom Gravy**

Made the same as Brown Gravy, but add **1 lb mushrooms, thinly sliced,** at the same time you add the onion.

Serves 6

Per serving: Calories: 137, Protein: 2 gm., Carbohydrates: 11 gm., Fat: 9 gm.

Biscuits can also be served with conserves, honey, maple syrup, Steins Syrup (see Mail Order Catalogs page 9), or molasses.

Breaded Tofu

■ ■

1 cup chick-pea flour
½ cup nutritional yeast flakes
½ cup arrowroot powder
1 teaspoon salt
cayenne to taste
2 lbs tofu, thinly sliced

This recipe reminds me of a breading my grand-mother used to put on things such as pork chops that she pan fried. This recipe has no cholesterol, but it sure takes me back home. This is a delicious, easy way to prepare tofu. Lemon juice is traditionally added to seafood dishes. It can also be a nice addition to the tofu.

Mix all of the dry ingredients together well. Dip each piece of tofu in the dry mix covering both sides, and pan fry in a hot, lightly oiled skillet. Sprinkle with lemon juice for a different flavor. You can make the flour mix in large amounts, store it in a container, and use it over and over again.

Serves 4 to 5

*Per serving: Calories: 338, Protein: 24 gm.,
Carbohydrates: 37 gm., Fat: 9 gm.*

Grits

▪▪

1 cup yellow grits
4 cups water
½ teaspoon salt

I don't use boxed grits. Instead, I use organic polenta that can be bought in bulk. My Grandmother always ate grits with sugar and milk. I like them with soymilk and honey. In Cajun country grits are usually served with eggs. Try serving these with the Scrambled Tofu (page 21).

Place the grits, water, and salt in a saucepan, bring to a boil, lower the heat to a simmer, and cook until desired thickness, stirring frequently. The grits will thicken after the heat is turned off, so it's a good idea to turn it off while they are a still a little thin. Some people like grits thin, some like them thick. It's your choice. They are good with a little cayenne sprinkled over the top served with sprouts.

Serves 4

Per serving: Calories: 146, Protein: 3 gm., Carbohydrates: 33 gm., Fat: 0 gm.

To use as a polenta casserole:
Cook to a thick consistency, pour in the bottom of a casserole dish, and top with your favorite soy cheese, Italian sauce, and sautéed vegetables.

Fried Grits

• •

1 cup left over grits, sliced
1 tablespoon oil
½ small onion, thinly sliced

This is a great recipe for any left over grits.

Slice the grits and fry in the oil with the onion.

Serves 2

Per serving: Calories: 147, Protein: 2 gm.,
Carbohydrates: 19 gm., Fat: 7 gm.

Coush Coush (cush cush)

• •

1½ cups corn flour
½ cup whole wheat pastry
 flour
1 teaspoon salt
2 teaspoons baking powder
1½ cups low-fat soymilk
1 tablespoon oil
1 tablespoon honey
⅓ cup oil

Here is an unusual, but very traditional, Cajun breakfast dish.

Mix all of the ingredients together well except the ⅓ cup oil. In a skillet, heat the ⅓ cup oil, and when the oil is hot add the mixture. Let it fry until a crust forms on the bottom. Stir and reduce to low heat. Cook for 15 minutes, stirring often until well cooked. It should resemble crumbled corn bread, only crunchy. Serve as a breakfast cereal with soymilk and honey.

Serves 4 to 6

Per serving: Calories: 353, Protein: 5 gm.,
Carbohydrates: 51 gm., Fat: 17 gm.

Pan Perdue (lost bread)

2½ cups soymilk
½ cup nutritional yeast flakes
1 teaspoon salt
½ cup whole wheat pastry
   flour
6 tablespoons arrowroot
   powder
2 tablespoons honey
¼ teaspoon vanilla
1 large stale sweet french
   bread, sliced ½ inch
   thick

This is what I grew up thinking was French toast. In Louisiana there is always an abundance of French bread, and when it gets stale there isn't much you can do with it. This is why it was called lost bread. If it wasn't used somehow it would be lost. MaMa prepared Pan Perdue often.

Mix together all of the ingredients except the bread. Dip the bread in the mixture, and soak for a few seconds. Pan fry in a hot, oiled skillet until golden on both sides. Serve with molasses or honey. We always used use Stein's Syrup which is a lot like molasses only not as strong.

Serves 4

Per serving: Calories: 435, Protein: 20 gm., Carbohydrates: 73 gm., Fat: 6 gm.

Chicory Coffee

4-12 tablespoons roasted
   ground chicory root
1 cup ground coffee

For many people the "morning call" wouldn't be complete without the chicory coffee.

Mix the chicory with the ground coffee before brewing. You can vary the flavor by increasing the amount of chicory.

Pancakes

■ ■

2 cups whole wheat pastry
   flour
¾ cup corn flour
3 teaspoons baking powder
½ teaspoon salt
¼ cup oil
2 cups soymilk or water
oil for frying

Mix all of the ingredients well, except the oil and fruit. Pour about 2 teaspoons of oil in a skillet, and place on a medium high heat. Pour ½ cup pancake batter in the hot skillet, and cook until the pancake begins to bubble and dry out on top. Serve with Steins Syrup or honey.

Serves 4

Per serving: Calories: 320, Protein: 12 gm., Carbohydrates: 59 gm., Fat: 4 gm.

bananas, thinly sliced
strawberries, thinly sliced
peaches, thinly sliced

Any one of these fruits can be added after the pancake has been poured.

Add the fruit to the top of the pancake, cook, flip, and cook until golden.

Variation ☛ ## Not Pigs in a Blanket

Pan fry pieces of Saucisse (page 19) in long strips, and place in the middle of each cooked pancake. Roll the pancake around the Saucisse, and hold them together with a toothpick. Serve as you would pancakes.

Serves 4 to 6

Per serving: Calories: 357 , Protein: 14 gm., Carbohydrates: 59 gm., Fat: 7 gm.

Saucisse

3 cups dry chick-peas
12 cups water for soaking
2 cups whole wheat pastry
  flour
1 cup rolled oats
1 cup nutritional yeast flakes
¾ cup sunflower oil
1 cup soymilk
2½ teaspoons salt
2 teaspoons garlic
2 teaspoons oregano
2 teaspoons fennel, crushed
2 teaspoons ground cloves
1 teaspoon cayenne
¼ cup soy sauce
2 tablespoons liquid smoke
2 tablespoons mustard

This recipe can be made with almost any legume, but I use chick-peas because of their wonderful flavor.

Bring the 12 cups of water to a boil, turn off the heat, and add the chick-peas. Soak overnight or for at least 6 hours. Drain and grind the soaked chick-peas in a food processor until very fine. In a large bowl, mix all of the dry ingredients. In a separate bowl, mix all of the wet ingredients. Add the chick-peas and the wet mix to the dry ingredients and mix well. Cut 4 pieces of aluminum foil 10 x 12-inches. Divide the mix into 4 equal parts, shape like sausages, and roll up in the foil. Seal the ends well, place in a steamer, and steam for 1 hour. Let cool. Slice into ¼-inch thick slices, and fry in a lightly oiled skillet until brown on both sides. This is a large recipe, and the leftovers freeze well.

Serves 24

Per serving: Calories: 203, Protein: 7 gm., Carbohydrates: 25 gm., Fat: 8 gm.

Fruit over Toast

■ ■

½ cup honey
5 peaches, thinly sliced, or
   3 cups of any of these fruits:
     apricots, thinly sliced
     whole blueberries
     figs, thinly sliced
     strawberries, thinly sliced
8 slices toast, of your choice

This is a very quick delicious breakfast.

In a saucepan, bring the honey to a boil, add the peaches, and simmer until the honey begins to thicken, stirring often. Spoon over toast.

Serves 4

Per serving: Calories: 316, Protein: 7 gm., Carbohydrates: 67 gm., Fat: 3 gm.

Peppered Tofu

■ ■

2 lbs tofu, thinly sliced
oil or frying
6 teaspoons paprika
½ teaspoon salt
¼ teaspoon cayenne
¼ teaspoon thyme

Slice the tofu into ¼-inch thick slices, and pan fry in a lightly oiled skillet until golden on both sides. In a small bowl, mix the remaining ingredients, and sprinkle each slice of tofu on both sides with the mixture. More or less salt or cayenne can be used to suit your own taste, or you can be creative and make up your own spice mixture. For easier sprinkling, the spice mixture can be placed in a shaker. This is a good snack food while traveling. The tofu can be placed in a container and is even better after it sets a while.

Serves 4 to 5

Per serving: Calories: 180, Protein: 14 gm., Carbohydrates: 4 gm., Fat: 12 gm.

Darkened Tofu

2 lbs tofu, cubed
3 tablespoons oil
⅓ cup tamari
⅛ teaspoon cayenne

In a large skillet, fry the tofu in the oil on medium high heat until the tofu is golden on all sides. Turn the heat off and let cool for 10 minutes. Add the tamari and cayenne, and cook on medium heat until the tamari begins to dry out. It is important to turn the tofu often so that it is thoroughly covered with the tamari.

Serves 4 to 6

Per serving: Calories: 221, Protein: 14 gm., Carbohydrates: 4 gm., Fat: 16 gm.

Scrambled Tofu

2 lbs tofu, mashed
2 tablespoons oil
1 teaspoon turmeric
¼ teaspoon salt
dash cayenne
½ cup green onions, minced

In a skillet, cook the tofu in the oil on medium high heat for 10 minutes. Add the remaining ingredients, except for the green onions, and cook until the tofu begins to dry out. The green onion should be sprinkled on just before the tofu is served. Scrambled tofu is similar to scrambled eggs and can be soft scrambled or hard scrambled. If the tofu is cooked long enough it will begin to brown.

Serves 4-6

Per serving: Calories: 187, Protein: 13 gm., Carbohydrates: 4 gm., Fat: 13 gm.

Fruit Preserves

8 cups whole strawberries, or any of the following fruits:
    whole figs
    peaches, thinly sliced
2 cups honey

Making fig and pear preserves was an annual event at our house. We had fig trees in the backyard which supplied us with enough figs to make preserves for the whole year. It is usually a good idea to cook enough preserves to last awhile. These recipes will last my family of four for one to two weeks.

Cook the honey and figs together on low heat until the syrup becomes thick, about 1½ hours, stirring often.

Makes 3 pints

Per 2 tablespoons: Calories: 51, Protein: 0 gm., Carbohydrates: 13 gm., Fat: 0 gm.

Pear Preserves

8 cups cooking pears, thinly sliced
2 cups honey
½ cup water
1 lemon thinly sliced

Cook the pears, honey, water, and lemon on low heat until the syrup becomes thick, about 1½ hours, stirring often. Apples or other fruit may be used in this recipe.

Makes 3 pints

Per 2 tablespoons: Calories: 55, Protein: 0 gm., Carbohydrates: 14 gm., Fat: 0 gm.

Watermelon Rind Preserves

rind of one small watermelon,
   thinly sliced
juice of 6 lemons
water to soak rind
2 cups honey
4 sticks of cinnamon
2 teaspoons cloves

Cut the watermelon rind into slices about ½ inch thick by 3 inches long, and place in a deep dish. The skin may be peeled or left on. Soak overnight in the lemon and enough water to cover the rind. Drain and put in a large pot. Add the remaining ingredients, and cook on medium low heat until the syrup becomes thick, about 1½ to 2 hours, stirring often.

Makes 3 pints

Per 2 tablespoons: Calories: 69, Protein: 0 gm.,
Carbohydrates: 17 gm., Fat: 0 gm.

Salads and Salad Dressings

Salad can be made ahead of time and stored in an airtight bag to keep it fresh. I make up enough salad and dressing to last a week. During the week all I have to do is add a main dish or vegetable or both. I find it very beneficial to have raw organic food as much as possible, and this is an easy and delicious way to do it. Check your local farmers market for inexpensive organic produce.

Avocado Salad

2 medium avocados, diced
1 medium tomato, diced
½ small red onion, thinly
  sliced
3 tablespoons fresh lemon
  juice
2 cloves garlic,
  finely shredded
2 tablespoons oil
¼ teaspoon salt
2 tablespoons parsley,
  minced
⅛ teaspoon cayenne

Mix all of the ingredients well; chill and serve.

Serves 4

*Per serving: Calories: 246, Protein: 2 gm.,
Carbohydrates: 16 gm., Fat: 18 gm.*

Carrot Raisin Salad

9 medium carrots, shredded
1½ cups raisins
2 tablespoons lemon juice
¼ cup fresh parsley, minced
4 tablespoons eggless
  mayonnaise
1 teaspoon honey
½ teaspoon salt

Shred the carrots with a food processor or by hand to
a medium shred, and set aside. In a separate bowl, mix
the remaining ingredients, add the carrots, and stir well.

Serves 4

*Per serving: Calories: 275, Protein: 2 gm.,
Carbohydrates: 57 gm., Fat: 3 gm.*

MaMa's Cole Slaw

5 cups green cabbage,
   thinly sliced
1 cup red cabbage, thinly
   sliced
2 carrots, shredded
½ small onion, minced
1 clove garlic, finely
   shredded
⅓ cup eggless mayonnaise
¼ teaspoon salt
½ teaspoon paprika
dash cayenne
1 tablespoon oil
1 tablespoon lemon juice
1 tablespoon honey

MaMa made the best cole slaw. It tasted like cabbage and a little dressing, not like mayonnaise.

Mix the green and red cabbage and carrots, and set aside. In a separate bowl, mix the remaining ingredients, add to the cabbage, and mix well.

Serves 6

Per serving: Calories: 99, Protein: 1 gm., Carbohydrates: 12 gm., Fat: 4 gm.

Cucumber Salad

3 medium cucumbers, thinly
   sliced
2 green onions, minced
1 large tomato, diced
3 tablespoons eggless
   mayonnaise
¼ teaspoon salt
dash cayenne

Wash the cucumbers well and cut off the ends. Do not peel. Rub down the sides with the points of a fork cutting the skin. This makes the cucumber more tender. My grandmother always said to rub both ends of the cucumber with the piece that you cut off to take out the bitterness. Add the remaining ingredients, stir well, and chill.

Serves 4

Per serving: Calories: 63, Protein: 1 gm., Carbohydrates: 8 gm., Fat: 2 gm.

Mixed Greens Salad

1 bunch spinach
1 small head green leaf
   lettuce
1 small romaine lettuce
½ lb mushrooms, thinly
   sliced
1 medium carrot, shredded
½ small red onion, thinly
   sliced
3 stalks celery, thinly sliced
1 bell pepper, thinly sliced

Wash the spinach and lettuce well, and break into large bite-size pieces. Add the remaining ingredients and mix well. Serve with your favorite dressing.

Serves 8

Per serving: Calories: 43, Protein: 2 gm., Carbohydrates: 6 gm., Fat: 0 gm.

French Potato Salad

8 medium potatoes, diced
1 small bell pepper, minced
1 small onion, minced
5 stalks celery, minced
¼ cup green onions, minced
3 tablespoons oil
¾ cup eggless mayonnaise
2 tablespoons mustard
1 teaspoon salt
½ teaspoon paprika
½ teaspoon turmeric
¼ teaspoon cayenne
¼ teaspoon garlic, finely
   shredded

Steam the potatoes until tender. Mix together the potatoes, bell peppers, onion, celery, and green onions, and set aside. In a separate bowl, mix the remaining ingredients, add to the vegetables, and mix well. Set aside and chill so the flavors can blend.

Serves 6 to 8

Per serving: Calories: 284, Protein: 2 gm., Carbohydrates: 38 gm., Fat: 12 gm.

Sweet Pea Salad

1 lb tofu, diced
1 tablespoon oil
2 lbs frozen peas (may be
   used defrosted only
   or lightly steamed)
3 stalks celery, minced
4 green onions, minced
½ cup eggless mayonnaise
¾ teaspoon salt
½ cup soy cheese, diced
   (optional)

This is a dish Mama always made on holidays. It is very simple and delicious.

Pan fry the tofu in the oil, add to the remaining ingredients, and mix well. Fresh peas may be used, but they must be steamed until just tender and then cooled

Serves 4 to 6

Per serving: Calories: 306, Protein: 15 gm., Carbohydrates: 33 gm., Fat: 11 gm.

Tofu Salad (mock egg salad)

1½ lbs tofu, mashed
½ small onion, minced
2 stalks celery, minced
¼ cup eggless mayonnaise
1 teaspoon salt
½ teaspoon turmeric
¼ teaspoon paprika
⅛ teaspoon cayenne

Mix all of the ingredients together, and chill. This is another dish that improves if it is allowed to set so the flavors can blend together.

Serves 4 to 6

Per serving: Calories: 139, Protein: 10 gm., Carbohydrates: 5 gm., Fat: 8 gm.

French Dressing

½ cup lemon juice
¾ cup oil
1 medium tomato, diced
2 green onions, chopped
2 tablespoons honey
1 teaspoon mustard
1 teaspoon salt
1 tablespoon paprika
1 tablespoon soy sauce
½ cup fresh parsley
½ cup water

This is a very tasty dressing. It only takes a little to enhance the flavor of the salad.

Combine all of the ingredients in a blender, chill, and serve. Keeps well in the refrigerator for 2 to 3 weeks.

Makes 2 cups

Per tablespoon: Calories: 52, Protein: 0 gm., Carbohydrates: 1 gm., Fat: 5 gm.

Donna's Vinaigrette Dressing

⅓ cup lemon juice
¾ cup oil
½ cup eggless mayonnaise
4 cloves garlic
¼ cup fresh parsley
1 teaspoon salt
½ cup water

My Mama always served salad with a vinaigrette dressing. This is my version.

Combine all of the ingredients in a blender, chill, and serve. Keeps well in the refrigerator.

Makes 2 cups

Per tablespoon: Calories: 54, Protein: 0 gm., Carbohydrates: 0 gm., Fat: 5 gm.

Soups and Sandwiches

Taunt Malute's Chili

3 cups dry pinto beans
1 cup textured vegetable
   protein
2 tablespoons oil
1 medium onion, minced
1 green bell pepper, minced
¼ cup fresh parsley
3 tablespoons chilli powder
2 teaspoons paprika
2 teaspoons salt
1½ teaspoons cumin
1 small jalapeño pepper,
   minced
¼ teaspoon cayenne
10 cups water

Soak the beans over night in enough water to cover at least 2 inches. Drain and set aside. Sauté the textured vegetable protein in the oil until it begins to brown, add the onions, and sauté an additional 10 minutes. Add the remaining ingredients, bring to a boil, lower to medium heat, and cook for 2 hours, stirring often. More water may be added to make the chili thinner.

Serves 6

Per serving: Calories: 213, Protein: 13 gm., Carbohydrates: 29 gm., Fat: 5 gm.

Navy Bean Soup

■ ■

1 lb dry navy beans
1 large onion, minced
3 stalks celery, minced
2 tablespoons oil
5 large tomatoes, diced
12 cups water
1½ teaspoons salt
2 teaspoons paprika
¼ teaspoon cayenne
2 bay leaves

This is a delicious soup that my grandmother often made.

Soak the beans overnight in enough water to cover 2 inches. Drain and set aside. In a large soup pot, sauté the onion and celery in the oil for 10 minutes, add the tomatoes, and sauté an additional 10 minutes. Add the remaining ingredients, bring to a boil, lower to a simmer, and cook for 2 hours.

Serves 6

Per serving: Calories: 162, Protein: 6 gm., Carbohydrates: 23 gm., Fat: 5 gm.

Potato Soup

∎∎∎∎∎∎∎∎∎∎∎∎∎∎∎∎∎∎∎∎∎∎∎∎∎∎∎∎∎∎∎∎∎∎∎∎

1 medium onion, minced
3 stalks celery, minced
2 tablespoons oil
10 cups water
6 large potatoes, diced
1½ teaspoons salt
1 teaspoon paprika

In a large soup pot, sauté the onion and celery in the oil for 10 minutes. Add the remaining ingredients, bring to a boil, and lower the heat to a simmer. Cook for 1½ hours, stirring often. If the soup gets too thick, add more water.

Serves 6

Per serving: Calories: 168, Protein: 2 gm.,
Carbohydrates: 30 gm., Fat: 4 gm.

Variations ☛ Other vegetables may be added to Potato Soup to give a little variety. Try one of these suggestions:

Make the Potato Soup and add **4 cups green beans, cut in ½-inch pieces,** at the same time the potatoes are added.

☛ Make the Potato Soup and add **1 lb spinach, diced large,** for the final 5 minutes. It's better if the spinach is barely cooked.

Corn Chowder

- -

4 cups fresh or frozen corn
3 cups soymilk
1 onion, minced
1 red bell pepper, minced
2 stalks celery, minced
2 tablespoons oil
2 potatoes, diced
3 cups water
1½ teaspoons salt
1 teaspoon paprika
⅛ teaspoon cayenne

Slice the fresh corn off the cob, and scrape each ear with the back of the knife. This removes the creamy part of the kernels left on the cob. Frozen corn may be used but fresh is better. Blend 2 cups of the corn in a blender with the soymilk, and set aside. Sauté the onion, bell pepper, and celery in the oil for 10 minutes, add the potatoes, and simmer for an additional 15 minutes, stirring often. Add the remaining ingredients, bring to a boil, lower the heat, and simmer for 1½ hours.

Serves 4 to 6

Per serving: Calories: 266, Protein: 7 gm., Carbohydrates: 41 gm., Fat: 8 gm.

Lima Bean Soup

- -

1 medium onion, diced
4 stalks celery, minced
1 small bell pepper, minced
2 tablespoons oil
8 cups water
1 lb small lima beans
1 clove garlic, minced
¼ teaspoon cayenne
1½ teaspoons salt
½ cup fresh parsley, minced

Mama always made this soup with pieces of ham. I love it without the ham. It's a delicious soup.

Sauté the onion, celery, and bell pepper in the oil for 5 minutes. Add the remaining ingredients, except for the parsley, bring to a boil, lower the heat to a simmer, and cook for about 1½ to 2 hours. Add the parsley, stir, and serve.

Serves 5 to 6

Per serving: Calories: 167, Protein: 6 gm., Carbohydrates: 24 gm., Fat: 5 gm.

Vegetable Soup

1 large onion, minced
3 stalks celery, thinly sliced
1 tablespoon oil
12 cups water
½ cup dry lima beans
3 potatoes, diced
2 carrots, thinly sliced
2 cups green beans, chopped
5 tomatoes, diced
2 cloves garlic, minced
1½ teaspoons salt
3 teaspoons paprika
¼ teaspoon cayenne
¼ lb spaghetti

In a large soup pot, sauté the onion and celery in the oil for 10 minutes. Add the remaining ingredients, except for the spaghetti, bring to a boil, lower the heat to a simmer, and cook for 1 hour. Add the spaghetti and cook for an additional ½ hour.

Serves 6 to 8

Per serving: Calories: 176, Protein: 5 gm., Carbohydrates: 34 gm., Fat: 2 gm.

Gumbo

7 cups okra
1 cup whole wheat pastry
   flour
¾ cup oil
1 medium onion, minced
1 large bell pepper, minced
4 stalks celery, minced
3 tomatoes, diced
10 cups water
1 tablespoon paprika
1 tablespoon salt
1 teaspoon filé
¼ teaspoon cayenne
filé to sprinkle on each bowl

In a dry skillet, fry the okra until lightly browned, and set aside. This takes the slime out of the okra. In a separate skillet, brown the flour and add the oil, stirring constantly, until it is a very dark brown (almost burnt). Don't be nervous, a very dark roux is the secret to good gumbo. When the roux is dark enough, immediately add the onion, bell pepper, celery, and tomatoes, and sauté for 10 minutes, stirring constantly. Add the okra, water, and spices, bring to a boil, lower to medium heat, and cook for 45 minutes. Hot water mixes more easily with the roux. Serve over brown rice, and sprinkle each bowl with about ¼ teaspoon filé.

Serves 6 to 8

Per serving: Calories: 325, Protein: 4 gm.,
Carbohydrates: 24 gm., Fat: 23 gm.

Dry Roux

whole wheat pastry flour

Gumbo can be made with what is called a dry roux, as opposed to a traditional roux made with flour and oil. This is good for those who are trying to cut back on fat. My mother says it is a good substitute, but I would be willing to bet that my grandmother, who would cook traditional style (were she still living), would disagree! It is a little different but still delicious.

Place the flour in a hot skillet on high heat. Stir constantly until the flour is a light brown. Immediately remove from the skillet to prevent the flour from burning. This can also be done in the oven. Preheat the oven to 350°. Place the flour on a large cookie sheet, and bake, stirring every 10 minutes, until the flour is light brown. Remove the flour from the cookie sheet as soon as it is browned to prevent the flour from burning. Dry roux can be made in large amounts so that some may be frozen for later use. My mother uses 5 pounds of flour at a time.

Gumbo With a Dry Roux

1 tablespoon oil
1 cup dry roux (page 37)
2 cups water

To make the Gumbo on page 36 with dry roux, sauté the onion, bell pepper, and celery in 1 tablespoon oil. Replace the browned flour and oil with the dry roux and water. Place the dry roux and water in a 1 quart mason jar with a tight fitting lid, and shake well until the roux is completely dissolved. Add to the sautéed vegetables. Everything else is the same.

Serves 6 to 8

Per serving: Calories: 122, Protein: 4 gm., Carbohydrates: 21 gm., Fat: 2 gm.

Gumbo Des Herbes

¾ cup whole wheat pastry
   flour
½ cup oil
2 large onions, minced
1 cup celery, minced
1 medium bell pepper,
   minced
6 cups water
12 cups greens, finely
   chopped (any combination
   of mustard greens, turnip
   greens, collards, or
   spinach)
1 cup fresh parsley, minced
½ teaspoon filé
½ teaspoon salt
¼ teaspoon cayenne

Brown the flour and add the oil, stirring constantly, until dark brown. Immediately add the onion, celery, and bell pepper and sauté for 10 minutes, stirring constantly. Add the remaining ingredients, bring to a boil, lower the heat, and simmer for 1½ hours.

Serves 6

*Per serving: Calories: 262, Protein: 5 gm.,
Carbohydrates: 20 gm., Fat: 18 gm.*

Variation ☞ For a lower fat version you can use a **dry roux**. In place of the whole wheat pastry flour and oil use:
1 cup dry roux (page 37)
2 cups water
¼ cup oil
Place the dry roux and water in a 1 quart mason jar with a tight fitting lid, and shake well until the roux is completely dissolved. Sauté the onion, bell pepper, and celery in the oil for 10 minutes. Add the roux mix and the remaining ingredients, bring to a boil, lower the heat, and simmer for 1½ hours.

Serves 6

*Per serving: Calories: 182, Protein: 5 gm.,
Carbohydrates: 20 gm., Fat: 9 gm.*

Po Boys

■ ■

4 (6-inch) French baguettes
3 tablespoons oil for buns
3 medium cloves garlic,
   finely shredded
1 medium onion, minced
⅓ cup oil
4 cups cooked brown rice
1 teaspoon salt
2 teaspoons paprika
½ cup whole wheat pastry
   flour
¼ cup eggless mayonnaise
5 cups mushrooms, thinly
   sliced
2 tablespoons oil
1 medium yellow onion,
   thinly sliced
1 medium red onion, thinly
   sliced
2 medium yellow bell
peppers, thinly sliced
3 medium green bell
   peppers, thinly
   sliced
1 teaspoon Cajun
   Seasoning (page 55)

These were originally made in Louisiana but were made with meat. They were so delicious that I decided to create a vegetarian version.

Slice the French baguettes length-ways down the middle. Mix the 3 tablespoons oil with the garlic, brush it on the bread, and grill in a skillet until golden brown. Spread the bread with the mayonnaise. Sauté the mushrooms in the 2 tablespoons of oil until they begin to look cooked but not brown. Add the onion, peppers, and Cajun Seasoning, and sauté until the onions become clear. Place ⅛ of the vegetables on each half baguette, and serve open-faced.

Serves 4 to 6

Per serving: Calories: 374, Protein: 9 gm., Carbohydrates: 41 gm., Fat: 18 gm.

Sloppy Joe's

2½ cups granular textured
  vegetable protein
2 tablespoons oil
1 medium onion, minced
1 medium bell pepper,
  minced
2½ cups water
6 tomatoes, diced
1 clove garlic, minced
2 teaspoons salt
⅛ teaspoon cayenne
2 tablespoons chilli powder
2 tablespoons honey
juice of 1 lemon
2 tablespoons soy sauce

My aunt started making these when I was a teen-ager. My grandmother loved them and made them often.

In a skillet, sauté the textured vegetable protein in the oil until lightly browned, stirring often. Add the onion, bell pepper, and tomatoes, and sauté for 20 minutes. Add the water and the remaining ingredients, stir well, and simmer for 30 minutes or until the mix begins to dry out. It should be really thick. Serve on a grilled whole grain burger or hot dog bun.

Serves 6 to 8

*Per serving (without bread): Calories: 182,
Protein: 16 gm., Carbohydrates: 20 gm., Fat: 3 gm.*

BBQ Sandwich

2 cups large chunk textured
  vegetable protein
1 medium bell pepper,
  minced
1 medium onion, minced
2 tablespoons oil
1 cup water
2 cloves of garlic, minced
½ teaspoon salt
⅛ teaspoon cayenne
2 cups Barbecue Sauce
  (page 47) or your favorite
  barbecue sauce

These are really delicious. I have an aunt in Texas who really thought these were barbecue beef sandwiches.

Sauté the textured vegetable protein, bell pepper, and onion in the oil for 10 minutes. Add the water, spices, and barbecue sauce, and simmer until the textured vegetable protein becomes tender, about 30 to 40 minutes. More water may be added if the textured vegetable protein seems a little tough. Serve on your favorite bun with potato salad.

Serves 6

*Per serving: Calories: 198, Protein: 15 gm.,
Carbohydrates: 23 gm., Fat: 5 gm.*

Rice Burger Patties

1 medium onion, minced
⅓ cup oil
4 cups cooked brown rice
1 teaspoon salt
2 teaspoons paprika
½ cup whole wheat pastry
   flour
oil for frying

In a skillet, sauté the onion in ⅓ cup oil for 15 minutes, stirring often. Add the remaining ingredients, except the flour, and mix well. Cook for an additional 15 minutes, stirring often. Add the flour and mix well. Let cool and form into 1-inch thick patties. Preheat the oven to 375°. If they fall apart easily add more flour; if they seem too dry add water a tablespoon at a time. Brush both sides with oil, and bake for 25 minutes or until golden. You can also fry them in about ¼ inch of hot oil in a skillet. You can use them for burgers or as a main course with gravy.

Serves 5

Per serving: Calories: 291, Protein: 6 gm., Carbohydrates: 50 gm., Fat: 7 gm.

Main Dishes

Gluten

■■■

Dry Ingredients:
2 cups instant gluten flour
(vital wheat gluten)
¼ cup whole wheat pastry
flour
¼ cup nutritional yeast
flakes
½ teaspoon salt
⅛ teaspoon cayenne
¼ teaspoon garlic powder
¼ teaspoon onion powder

Wet Ingredients:
2 tablespoons tamari
1½ cups water

Gluten Broth:
¼ cup tamari
3 cloves garlic
¼ medium onion, thinly
sliced
½ large bell pepper, thinly
sliced
¼ teaspoon cayenne
enough water to cover
gluten (6-8 cups)

In a large bowl, mix the dry ingredients together. In a separate bowl, mix the wet ingredients together, pour them over the dry, and mix well. Add more water if the mixture still has dry flour around the edges. It will become very stiff, but don't be alarmed: this is gluten. Break or cut it into 3 or 4 pieces, place in a large pot, cover with at least 3 inches of water, and add the gluten broth. Boil for 45 minutes. Serve in any way you would beef or chicken. Gluten can be sliced, or left whole and stuffed with garlic, as you would a roast. Freezes well.

Serves 8

*Per serving: Calories: 92, Protein: 11 gm.,
Carbohydrates: 7 gm., Fat: 2 gm.*

Creole Gluten

■■■

½ medium onion, minced
½ medium bell pepper, minced
1 stalk celery, minced
¼ cup oil
2 cloves garlic, minced
3 medium tomatoes, diced
2 tablespoons fresh parsley, minced
½ teaspoon salt
1 teaspoon paprika
½ teaspoon filé
⅛ teaspoon cayenne
1 bay leaf
3 tablespoons water
1 recipe Gluten (page 45), thinly sliced or cubed

Simmer the onion, bell pepper, and celery in the oil for 15 minutes. Add the remaining ingredients, except for the gluten, and simmer for 30 minutes, stirring often. Cut the gluten into 1-inch strips, and add to the sauce. Simmer for an additional 20 minutes, stirring often. More water may be added if the sauce seems too thick. Serve over brown rice or by itself.

Serves 8

Per serving: Calories: 240, Protein: 31 gm., Carbohydrates: 12 gm., Fat: 8 gm.

Barcecue Gluten

Barbecue Sauce:
½ medium onion, minced
2 tablespoons oil
2 cloves garlic, minced
4 cups tomato sauce
¼ cup water
¼ cup honey
2 tablespoons molasses
¼ cup mustard
1 teaspoon salt
1 teaspoon allspice
¼ teaspoon cayenne
2 tablespoons fresh parsley, minced
1½ tablespoons tamari
2¼ teaspoons liquid smoke

1 recipe Gluten (page 45), thinly sliced

Simmer the onion in the oil for 10 minutes. Add the remaining ingredients, except the gluten, bring to a boil, lower the heat, and simmer for 1 hour. Preheat the oven to 350°. Slice the gluten into rib size slices, and dip into the barbecue sauce. Place in a rectangle baking dish, and bake for 30 minutes. Brush with more sauce, and bake for an additional 20 minutes. May also be cooked on a barbecue grill.

Serves 8

Per serving: Calories: 259, Protein: 12 gm., Carbohydrates: 36 gm., Fat: 6 gm.

Cajun Tofu or Eggplant

1 medium onion, thinly sliced
2 medium bell peppers, thinly sliced
2 stalks celery, thinly sliced
¼ cup oil (you can use half the oil if you use the tofu)
2 small eggplants, or 2 lbs tofu, cubed
2 medium tomatoes, diced
½ cup fresh parsley, minced
1 teaspoon salt
2 teaspoons paprika
¾ teaspoon thyme
½ teaspoon filé
¼ teaspoon cayenne
⅓ cup water

Sauté the onion, bell pepper, and celery in the oil for 5 minutes. Add the tofu or eggplant cubes, and sauté until they begin to brown. Add the remaining ingredients, and simmer on low heat for 45 minutes. Serve as a side dish or over rice.

Serves 4 to 6

Per serving (with tofu): Calories: 342, Protein: 26 gm., Carbohydrates: 14 gm., Fat: 19 gm.

Per serving (with eggplant): Calories: 136, Protein: 2 gm., Carbohydrates: 19 gm., Fat: 5 gm.

Vegetable Stew and Dumplings

■■

1 medium onion, diced
3 stalks celery, thinly sliced
1 medium bell pepper, diced
2 tablespoons oil
5 tablespoons whole wheat
   pastry flour
1 cup water
3 medium potatoes, diced
2 carrots, thinly sliced
1 cup green beans, chopped
½ cup peas, fresh or frozen
2 medium tomatoes, diced
3 green onions, minced
1 teaspoon salt
2 teaspoons paprika
¼ teaspoon cayenne
½ Biscuit recipe (page 12)
2 cups water

Sauté the onion, celery, and bell pepper in the oil for a few minutes. In a dry skillet, brown the flour until light brown, stirring constantly. Place the browned flour and 1 cup water in a quart mason jar with a tight fitting lid, and shake well until the flour is completely dissolved. Add the sautéed vegetables and the remaining ingredients, and cook on low heat for 45 minutes. Roll out the biscuit dough ½ inch thick, and slice into strips ¼ by 2 inches. Place the dumplings on top of the stew, and cook uncovered for 10 minutes. Cover and cook for an additional 10 minutes. More water may be added if the sauce gets too thick. Serve over brown rice.

Serves 6

Per serving: Calories: 313, Protein: 7 gm., Carbohydrates: 49 gm., Fat: 10 gm.

Cornbread Dressing

■■■

1 lb tofu, diced
2 tablespoons oil
1 recipe Cornbread
  (page 13), crumbled
  (approximately 3 cups)
4 cups mushrooms, thinly
  sliced
⅓ cup oil
1 large onion, minced
1 large bell pepper, minced
4 stalks celery, minced
1 teaspoon salt
1 teaspoon paprika
⅛ to ¼ teaspoon cayenne

In a skillet, sauté the tofu in 2 tablespoons oil until the tofu is golden. In a separate bowl, mix the tofu with the crumbled cornbread. Sauté the mushrooms in ⅓ cup oil until they begin to brown. Add the onion, bell pepper, and celery, and sauté for 15 minutes. Add the spices and simmer an additional 25 minutes, stirring often. Mix with the cornbread and tofu, adding a little water or gravy if it seems too dry. Serve with Brown Gravy (page 13).

Serves 6 to 8

Per serving: Calories: 320, Protein: 10 gm., Carbohydrates: 29 gm., Fat: 17 gm.

Pecan Rice Dressing

1 large onion, minced
3 green onions, minced
3 stalks celery, minced
1 large green pepper,
  minced
⅓ cup oil
2 cups pecans, chopped
2 teaspoons paprika
1 teaspoon ground cumin
½ teaspoon thyme
½ teaspoon oregano
1½ teaspoons salt
⅛ teaspoon cayenne
4 cups cooked brown rice

Sauté the onions, celery, and bell pepper in the oil for 15 minutes. Add the remaining ingredients, except the rice, and simmer for another 15 minutes. Stir in the rice and cook on low heat for 10 minutes, stirring often.

Serves 6 to 8

Per serving: Calories: 376, Protein: 6 gm., Carbohydrates: 39 gm., Fat: 22 gm.

Dirty Rice

■■■

4 tablespoons flour
1 medium onion, chopped
2 stalks celery, minced
2 green bell peppers,
  minced
3 cups fresh mushrooms,
  minced
3 tablespoons oil
3 teaspoons oil
¾ cup textured vegetable
  protein granules
1½ cups water
½ cup fresh parsley,
  minced
4 cups cooked brown rice
2 teaspoons filé
1½ teaspoons salt
½ teaspoon paprika
¼ teaspoon cayenne

In a dry skillet, brown the flour, stirring constantly, until light brown in color. In a separate skillet, sauté the onion, celery, and bell pepper, in 3 tablespoons of oil for 10 minutes, stirring constantly. Add to the flour and mix well. Brown the mushrooms in 3 teaspoons of oil. Add the textured vegetable protein, and brown well with the mushrooms for 10 minutes. Add to the onion and flour mixture, and sauté for another 10 minutes. Add the water and simmer for 10 minutes, stirring often. The mixture should be fairly thick, and the textured vegetable protein should be tender and chewy. If it is not tender add more water, ¼ cup at a time. Add the remaining ingredients, mix well, and serve.

Serves 6

*Per serving: Calories: 312, Protein: 10 gm.,
Carbohydrates: 45 gm., Fat: 10 gm.*

Dupois' Cabbage Rolls

■■

Sauce:
½ medium onion, minced
2 tablespoons oil
6 medium tomatoes, diced
 or 1 (32 ounce) can
 tomato sauce
1½ teaspoons salt
2 teaspoons paprika sauce
¼ teaspoon cayenne

1 very large head cabbage
1 medium onion, minced
2 tablespoons oil
3 green onions, minced
2 medium cloves garlic,
 minced
⅓ cup textured vegetable
 protein
⅓ cup water
2 medium tomatoes, diced
4 cups cooked brown rice
⅓ cup fresh parsley,
 minced
2 teaspoons salt
2 teaspoons paprika
¼ teaspoon cayenne

Dupois (pronounced due-poy) was the name of my grandmother (MaMa) before her marriage to my grandfather (Pop). I named these after her because she made the best Cabbage Rolls, and I just imagine that perhaps she knew how to make them before she met Pop.

First, make the sauce by sautéing the onion in 2 tablespoons of oil. Add the tomatoes, salt, paprika, and cayenne, bring to a boil, and simmer for 1 hour.

Remove the core of the cabbage, and steam the whole head in a large pot with the core side down until it will separate, about 20 minutes. Remove and let cool. In a large skillet, sauté the onion in 2 tablespoons of oil for about 10 minutes, stirring often. Add the green onions, garlic, textured vegetable protein, water, and tomatoes, and simmer for 15 minutes. Add the rice and spices, and mix well. Preheat the oven to 350°. Carefully separate the cabbage, one leaf at a time, and cut out the core pieces. Place some of the rice mixture on each leaf. Leave enough room to fold the sides inward, and roll up the leaves. Place the cabbage rolls in a casserole dish, and cover with the sauce. Bake for 30 minutes.

Serves 6

Per serving: Calories: 355, Protein: 9 gm., Carbohydrates: 57 gm., Fat: 10 gm.

Fried Veggie Platter

■■

1 lb broccoli
1 lb cauliflower
1 lb whole button
   mushrooms
2 small zucchini, thinly
   sliced
2 carrots, thinly sliced
1 large onion, sliced
   ½ inch thick
4 cups chick-pea flour
1⅛ teaspoons Cajun
   Seasoning (page 55)
2½ cups water
oil for frying

In all of the restaurants in Cajun country, they serve a fried seafood platter. Here is my version of that famous dish.

Break the broccoli and the cauliflower into flowerets, and prepare the rest of the vegetables. Place the flour and Cajun Seasoning in a large bowl, and mix well. Dip all of the vegetables in the dry flour mixture, and set aside. Add the water to the flour, and stir well (the mixture should resemble a thick pancake batter). More water may be added to thin out the batter, or more flour may be added if the batter is too thick. Dip each veggie into the liquid flour mixture, and deep fry. The oil should be very hot and at least 1 to 1½ inches deep. Place the vegetables on a paper bag to drain the oil.

Serves 6 to 8

Per serving: Calories: 402, Protein: 15 gm., Carbohydrates: 55 gm., Fat: 13 gm.

Cajun Dip

■■■

2 cups eggless mayonnaise
2 tablespoons paprika
¼ teaspoon cayenne
2 cloves garlic, finely
   shredded
1 teaspoon oil
3 tablespoons tamari
¼ cup water

Mix all of the ingredients together well. Serve in small dipping dishes with the Fried Veggie Platter (page 54). More water may be added for a thinner sauce.

Makes 2½ cups

Per tablespoon: Calories: 41, Protein: 0 gm., Carbohydrates: 1 gm., Fat: 4 gm.

Cajun Seasoning

■■■

3 cups salt
¼ cup chili powder
⅓ cup cayenne
¼ cup garlic powder

This is a combination of spices that can be made in large amounts. It can be used in place of the salt and cayenne in any of these recipes. My Mama uses it in almost all of her cooking.

Mix all of the ingredients together, and place in a shaker.

Cajun Meatless Patties

1½ cups walnut meal
1 cup sunflower seed meal
3½ cups cooked lentils
1½ cups toasted bread
  crumbs
1 medium onion, minced
4 cloves garlic, minced
1 medium bell pepper,
  minced
2 tablespoons oil
1 teaspoon salt
2 teaspoons paprika
½ teaspoon oregano
¼ teaspoon filé
¼ teaspoon thyme
¼ teaspoon cayenne

Chop the walnuts and sunflower seeds in the blender until they are a fine meal. Mix with the lentils and toasted bread crumbs. Preheat the oven to 350°. In a skillet, sauté the onions, garlic, and bell pepper in the oil for 15 minutes, and add to the lentils. Add the remaining ingredients, and mix well. Form into 1-inch thick by 3-inch wide patties, and place on an oiled cookie sheet. Brush the tops with oil, and bake for 40 minutes or until golden. These patties are delicious served with Brown Mushroom Gravy (page 13).

Serves 6 to 8

Per serving: Calories: 478, Protein: 16 gm., Carbohydrates: 46 gm., Fat: 24 gm.

Creole Courtboullion (coo-bee-yon)

■ ■

2 lbs tempeh or tofu, sliced
  ¼ inch thick
¼ cup oil (you can use
  ½ the oil for frying if
  using tofu)
1 medium onion, minced
3 cloves garlic, minced
1 medium bell pepper,
  minced
2 stalks celery, minced
1 teaspoon salt
¾ teaspoon filé
¼ teaspoon cayenne
2 bay leaves
6 medium tomatoes, diced
⅓ cup water
½ lemon, thinly sliced
¼ cup fresh parsley, minced

Frying tempeh requires more oil than frying tofu. If you use tofu, you can lower the fat content by frying it in less oil. Just flip often to avoid sticking.

Pan fry the tofu or tempeh in half of the oil until golden. Set aside. Sauté the onion, garlic, bell pepper, celery, and spices in the remaining oil. Stir well, lower the heat, and simmer for 5 minutes. Add the tomatoes and water, and simmer for 30 minutes. Add the tofu or tempeh, lemon, and parsley, and simmer for 25 minutes, stirring carefully. Serve over hot brown rice.

Serves 6 to 8

Per serving (with tofu): Calories: 203, Protein: 110 gm., Carbohydrates: 10 gm., Fat: 13 gm.

Per serving (with tempeh): Calories: 363, Protein: 22 gm., Carbohydrates: 30 gm., Fat: 17 gm.

Jambalaya (jum-ba-lie-ya)

■■■

1½ cups tofu, crumbled
2 teaspoons oil
½ cup textured vegetable
  protein
1 tablespoon oil
1 medium, onion minced
1 large bell pepper, minced
3 stalks celery, minced
2 tomatoes, diced
3 cloves garlic, minced
1 teaspoon salt
1 teaspoon paprika
1 teaspoon cumin powder
1 teaspoon filé
¼ teaspoon cayenne
½ cup water
5 cups cooked brown rice

In a skillet, brown the tofu in 2 teaspoons of oil until golden, and set aside. In the same skillet, sauté the textured vegetable protein with 1 tablespoon of oil until it begins to brown. Add the tofu and the remaining ingredients, except the water and rice. Sauté for 15 minutes, add the water, and simmer on low heat for 20 minutes, stirring often. Add the rice and simmer for an additional 10 minutes, stirring well and often.

Serves 8

Per serving: Calories: 238, Protein: 9 gm., Carbohydrates: 37 gm., Fat: 5 gm.

Potato Stew

■■■

5 medium potatoes, diced
1 medium onion, minced
1 small bell pepper, minced
2 tablespoons oil
½ cup fresh parsley,
  minced
1 cup low-fat soymilk
1 teaspoon salt
½ teaspoon paprika
⅛ teaspoon cayenne

This must have been one of MaMa's favorites, because I remember having it often, and I just loved it.

Steam the potatoes until tender, and set aside. Sauté the onion and bell pepper in the oil for 5 minutes, add the potatoes, and sauté for an additional 10 minutes, stirring often. Add the remaining ingredients, and simmer on low heat for 30 minutes, stirring often. More water may be added for a thinner sauce. This was always served over rice.

Serves 5

Per serving: Calories: 196, Protein: 3 gm., Carbohydrates: 31 gm., Fat: 6 gm.

Louisiana Spaghetti

1½ lbs spaghetti of your
  choice
water for boiling spaghetti
2 tablespoons oil
½ teaspoon salt
1 medium onion, minced
1 large bell pepper, thinly
  sliced
3 tablespoons oil
10 medium tomatoes, diced
10 cloves garlic, minced
1 teaspoon salt
1 tablespoon basil
2 teaspoons paprika
1 teaspoon oregano
½ teaspoon rosemary
½ teaspoon thyme
¼ teaspoon cayenne
½ cup water
¼ cup nutritional yeast
  flakes

In a large pot, add enough water to cover the spaghetti with 2 inches of water, ½ teaspoon salt, and 2 tablespoons oil, and bring to a boil. Add the spaghetti and cook until tender stirring often. When done, rinse the spaghetti in a colander with hot water, and set aside. In a large skillet, sauté the onion and bell pepper in 3 tablespoons oil, and add the remaining ingredients, except the spaghetti. Cook on low heat for 45 minutes, stirring often. Mix the spaghetti with the sauce, and serve.

Serves 6 to 8

Per serving: Calories: 258, Protein: 8 gm., Carbohydrates: 41 gm., Fat: 7 gm.

Pepper Dressing

1 cup textured vegetable protein
2 tablespoons oil
4 large bell peppers, minced
1 medium onion, minced
5 green onions, minced
1 teaspoon salt
2 teaspoons paprika
⅛ teaspoon cayenne
¾ cup water
1 lb mushrooms, thinly sliced
2 tablespoons oil
5 cups cooked brown rice
1 jalapeño pepper, finely shredded

Pan fry the textured vegetable protein in 2 tablespoons oil until it begins to brown. Add the bell peppers, onions, and seasonings, and sauté for 10 minutes, stirring often. Add the water and simmer for 20 minutes, stirring often. Sauté the mushrooms in 2 tablespoons of oil until they begin to brown, about 15 minutes. Add the mushrooms, rice, and jalapeño pepper to the textured vegetable protein mixture, and stir well. Heat on very low heat until the rice is hot throughout, and serve.

Serves 8

Per serving: Calories: 268, Protein: 9 gm., Carbohydrates: 40 gm., Fat: 7 gm.

Eggplant Dressing

1 lb tofu, diced
¼ cup oil
1 large onion, diced
3 green onions, minced
1 large green pepper,
  minced
1 stalk celery, minced
3 medium tomatoes, diced
2 medium eggplants, diced
3 cloves garlic, minced
2 teaspoons paprika
½ teaspoon thyme
1¼ teaspoons Cajun
  Seasoning (page 55)
2 cups cooked brown rice
1 cup bread crumbs

Sauté the tofu in the oil until it begins to brown. Add the onions, green pepper, celery, tomatoes, and eggplant, and sauté for 25 minutes, stirring often. Add the seasonings and rice, and simmer for an additional 15 minutes, stirring often. Add the bread crumbs and stir well. Simmer an additional 10 minutes, and serve.

Serves 6 to 8

Per serving: Calories: 304, Protein: 9 gm., Carbohydrates: 40 gm., Fat: 11 gm.

Red Beans and Rice

2 cups dry red kidney beans
   water for soaking beans
1 large onion, minced
4 stalks celery, minced
1 large green bell pepper,
   minced
1 tablespoon oil
3 cloves garlic, minced
2 jalapeño peppers, minced
1¾ teaspoons Cajun
   Seasoning (page 55)
4 bay leaves
½ teaspoon thyme
8 cups water for cooking
   beans
6 cups cooked brown rice

Soak the beans overnight, or at least 6 hours, in a large container with enough water to cover them with 2 inches of water. Drain well before cooking. In a large pot, sauté the onion, celery, and bell pepper in the oil for 15 minutes, then add the remaining ingredients, except the brown rice. Bring to a boil, and lower to a simmer, stirring often. Simmer for 1¼ hours or until the beans begin to break up, and the liquid becomes saucy like a gravy. Serve over brown rice.

Serves 6 to 8

Per serving: Calories: 356, Protein: 12 gm., Carbohydrates: 69 gm., Fat: 2 gm.

Smothered Okra Over Rice

5 cups okra, thinly sliced
1 medium onion, diced
3 tablespoons oil
4 cloves garlic, minced
4 medium tomatoes, diced
1 teaspoon salt
¼ teaspoon cayenne
5 cups cooked brown rice

In a dry skillet, fry the okra until it begins to brown, and set aside. This takes the slime out of the okra. In a separate pan, sauté the onion in the oil for 15 minutes, add the garlic and tomatoes, and simmer for an additional 30 minutes. Add the spices and the okra, and simmer for ½ hour or until the okra becomes tender. Serve over brown rice.

Serves 6

Per serving: Calories: 308, Protein: 6 gm., Carbohydrates: 53 gm., Fat: 7 gm.

Blackened Tofu

Seasoning mixture:
6 teaspoons onion powder
6 teaspoons garlic powder
1 teaspoons cayenne
6 teaspoons filé
½ teaspoon salt

2 lbs tofu, sliced ½ inch
   thick
oil for dipping tofu

In a bowl, combine the seasoning mixture. Dip the tofu in the oil and then in the seasoning mixture. Fry in a hot iron skillet until blackened on both sides.

Serves 6

Per serving: Calories: 195, Protein: 11 gm., Carbohydrates: 3 gm., Fat: 15 gm.

Stuffed Peppers

4 large green bell peppers
2 stalks celery, minced
1 small onion, minced
2 tablespoons oil
2 cloves garlic, minced
8 slices whole wheat bread,
  toasted and cubed
2 cups cooked brown rice
¼ cup fresh parsley,
  minced
1 teaspoon salt
1 teaspoon paprika
¼ teaspoon filé
⅛ teaspoon cayenne
2 slices whole wheat bread,
  toasted and blended into
  crumbs

MMM! Another of MaMa's great recipe's vegan style.

Slice the tops off the bell peppers, remove the seeds and stems, mince the tops, and set aside. Place the hollow bell peppers in 2 inches of water in a saucepan large enough to hold all 4 peppers. Simmer with the lid on for 15 minutes, and set aside. In a large skillet, sauté the celery, onion, and bell pepper tops in the oil for 20 minutes, stirring often. Add the garlic and simmer for 5 more minutes. Preheat the oven to 350°. Briefly dip the toasted bread in water, and gently squeeze out any excess moisture. Add the bread, brown rice, parsley, and spices, and stir well. Stuff the bell peppers with the mixture, and sprinkle the bread crumbs on top of the stuffed peppers. Place ¼ cup water in an oven pan with the peppers, and bake for 25 minutes.

Serves 4

Per serving: Calories: 385, Protein: 11 gm., Carbohydrates: 61 gm., Fat: 10 gm.

Vegetable Etoufee (ay-too-fay)

■■■

1 lb broccoli flowerets
(about 5 cups)
1 lb cauliflower flowerets
(about 5 cups)
4 tablespoons whole wheat
pastry flour
3 tablespoons oil
1 medium onion, thinly
sliced
2 carrots, thinly sliced
1 medium bell pepper,
thinly sliced
2 stalks celery, thinly sliced
2 tomatoes, diced
½ cup tomato sauce
1 teaspoon salt
2 teaspoons paprika
¼ teaspoon cayenne
1 cup water
½ cup soy cheese, grated

Lightly steam the broccoli and cauliflower, and set aside. In a skillet, heat the flour and oil together on medium heat, stirring constantly until the flour becomes golden brown. Immediately add the onion, bell pepper, and celery, lower the heat, and simmer for 10 minutes, stirring often. Add the remaining ingredients, except the soy cheese, bring to a boil, lower the heat, and simmer for 20 minutes. Add the soy cheese and simmer another 10 minutes. May be served over brown rice.

Serves 5

*Per serving: Calories: 217, Protein: 6 gm.,
Carbohydrates: 20 gm., Fat: 13 gm.*

Vegetable Boulettes (meatless balls)

2 cups potatoes, shredded
2 cups broccoli, shredded
2 cups cauliflower, shredded
¼ onion, shredded
1 cup chick-pea flour or
  whole wheat pastry flour
½ teaspoon salt
oil for frying

Mix all of the ingredients together, and form into 2-inch balls or 1-inch thick patties. If necessary, add more flour to make them stick together. Cook in hot oil about ½ inch deep, turning carefully until golden on all sides. For baking, add ¼ cup oil to the ingredients, and mix well. Brush each patty with oil on both sides, and bake at 350° until golden, approximately 40 minutes. Serve with Brown Gravy (page 13), with spaghetti dishes, or as an appetizer. Other vegetables, such as eggplant, rhubarb, etc., may be used to replace 1 cup of the cauliflower or potatoes. Use your imagination.

Makes 12 balls

*Per ball: Calories: 121, Protein: 2 gm.,
Carbohydrates: 17 gm., Fat: 4 gm.*

Sweet Boulettes

■■■

3 cups yams, shredded
1 cup potatoes, shredded
1½ cups carrots, shredded
¼ onion, shredded
1 cup chick-pea flour or
   whole wheat pastry flour
½ teaspoon salt
oil for frying

Mix all of the ingredients together, and form into 2-inch balls or 1-inch thick patties. If necessary, add more flour to make them stick together. Cook in hot oil about ½ inch deep, turning carefully until golden on all sides. For baking, add ¼ cup oil to the ingredients, and mix well. Brush each patty with oil on both sides, and bake at 350° until golden, approximately 40 minutes. Boulettes can be served with Brown Gravy (page 13) or as an appetizer. Other vegetables, such as eggplant, may be used to replace 1 cup of the carrots or potatoes. Use your imagination.

Makes 15 balls

*Per ball: Calories: 111, Protein: 2 gm.,
Carbohydrates: 18 gm., Fat: 3 gm.*

Side Dishes and Sauces

Broussard Black-Eyed Peas

1 onion, minced
1 bell pepper, minced
2 stalks celery, minced
1 tablespoon oil
2 cups dry black-eyed peas
⅓ cup green onions,
   minced
⅓ cup fresh parsley minced
¾ teaspoon salt
¼ teaspoon cayenne
8 cups water

We always had this dish on New Year's day. Mamma said it brought good luck, and everyone had to eat some.

In a 4-quart soup pot, sauté the onion, bell pepper, and celery in the oil. Add the remaining ingredients, bring to a boil, and lower the heat to a simmer. Cook for about 45 minutes until the black-eyed peas are soft and the liquid is creamy. More liquid may be added for a thinner sauce. A delicious dish served with Corn Bread (page 90).

Serves 4 to 6

Per serving: Calories: 147, Protein: 7 gm., Carbohydrates: 23 gm., Fat: 3 gm.

Lafayette Lima Beans

1 onion, minced
1 tablespoon oil
8 cups water
2 cups dry lima beans
1 small bell pepper, minced
4 cloves garlic, minced
1 teaspoon salt
¼ teaspoon cayenne

This is a favorite of Cajun grandmothers.

In a 4-quart pot, sauté the onion in the oil for 10 minutes, stirring often. Add the remaining ingredients, bring to a boil, lower the heat to a simmer, and cook for an additional 45 minutes. They should be real juicy, so if necessary, add more water. This is a delicious dish served with Corn Bread (page 90).

Serves 4 to 6

*Per serving: Calories: 153, Protein: 7 gm.,
Carbohydrates: 25 gm., Fat: 3 gm.*

Bayou Teche Candied Yams

▪▪▪

½ cup honey
¼ cup molasses
2 tablespoons oil
⅛ teaspoon salt
1 teaspoon cinnamon
6 medium yams, cubed
½ cup chopped walnuts or
  pecans

Using a candy thermometer, heat the honey and molasses to 260°. You can also cook it for about 10 minutes, put a few drops of the honey and molasses into a dish of cold water, and when it feels medium hard, it is done. Preheat the oven to 350°. Add the oil, salt, and cinnamon, and mix well. Pour over the potatoes, add the nuts, and bake for 45 minutes or until tender.

Serves 6

*Per serving: Calories: 395, Protein: 3 gm.,
Carbohydrates: 73 gm., Fat: 10 gm.*

Cauliflower Au Gratin

1 large cauliflower, broken
    into flowerets
½ medium onion, minced
1 tablespoon oil
½ teaspoon salt
dash of cayenne
3 tablespoons fresh parsley,
    minced
1½ cups Yeast Cheese Sauce
    (page 84), or soy cheddar
    cheese, shredded
⅓ cup low-fat soymilk

Preheat the oven to 350°. Lightly steam the cauliflower and set aside. Sauté the onion in the oil for 5 minutes, add the cauliflower, and simmer an additional 5 minutes. Place the sautéed vegetables, salt, cayenne, and parsley in a baking dish, mix, and cover with the cheese and soymilk. Bake for 15 minutes or until the cheese becomes melted and bubbly.

Serves 4 to 6

Per serving: Calories: 163, Protein: 10 gm., Carbohydrates: 20 gm., Fat: 5 gm.

French Fried Okra

2 lbs okra
2½ cups chick-pea flour
½ cup corn flour
½ teaspoon salt
¼ teaspoon paprika
⅛ teaspoon cayenne
1¼ cups water
oil for frying

Slice the okra into ½-inch pieces. In a bowl, mix 1 cup of the chick-pea flour and the okra. In a separate bowl, mix the remaining ingredients with enough water to make a fairly thick batter. Drop the okra into the batter, and stir together gently. Take the okra, either piece by piece or in spoonfuls, and drop into 2 inches of hot oil. Fry until golden on both sides. Place on a paper bag to drain.

Serves 4

Per serving: Calories: 385, Protein: 12 gm., Carbohydrates: 53 gm., Fat: 12 gm.

French Fried Onion Rings

2 large onions, sliced
3 cups chick-pea flour
1 cup water
½ teaspoon salt
¼ teaspoon paprika
⅛ teaspoon cayenne
oil for frying

Slice the onions into ¼-inch slices, and separate into rings. Take 1 cup of the chick-pea flour, and sprinkle over the sliced onions. Mix the remaining ingredients adding enough water to make a fairly thick batter. Dip each onion ring into the batter, and place in two inches of hot oil. Fry each side until golden. Place on a paper bag to drain. The amount of batter needed will depend on the size of the onion. Salt and pepper to taste.

Serves 4

*Per serving: Calories: 361, Protein: 13 gm.,
Carbohydrates: 45 gm., Fat: 13 gm.*

Southern Potatoes

3 tablespoons oil
4 large potatoes, thinly sliced
1 medium onion, thinly sliced
1 teaspoon salt
1 teaspoon paprika
⅛ teaspoon cayenne
¾ cup water
2 green onions, minced

In a large skillet, heat the oil on high heat. When the oil is hot, add the potatoes, and fry until brown on one side, flip over, and brown again. Keep flipping until all the potatoes seem to be done and somewhat brown. Add the onion, salt, paprika, and cayenne, and simmer for 10 minutes, stirring often. Stir by flipping with a spatula, not a spoon, or the potatoes may get mashed. Add the water and flip the potatoes again. Cook on low heat, flipping often, until the liquid thickens. Sprinkle the green onions on top, and serve.

Serves 5

*Per serving: Calories: 223, Protein: 2 gm.,
Carbohydrates: 35 gm., Fat: 8 gm.*

Dwayne's Julienne French Fries

oil for frying
6 large potatoes, cut into
   ¼ by ¼-inch strips
salt to taste
cayenne to taste

Our oldest son perfected this recipe. He loves fries and always had such patience with cutting them up and frying them perfectly.

In a 9-inch skillet, place 2 inches of oil on high heat until the oil is hot. Fill the skillet with potatoes about 1 inch deep. Be careful when adding the potatoes. As they begin to fry separate them gently (do this often), and turn them over when they are brown on the first side. Cook on the other side until golden. When adding more potatoes, be sure the oil is still 2 inches deep and very hot. The secret to this recipe is patience and a desire for french fries. When properly done they should be golden on all sides. Separating them helps accomplish this. When the potatoes are done, place them on a brown bag or in a colander to drain. Sprinkle with salt and cayenne, and shake to be sure the seasoning is evenly distributed.

Serves 4

Per serving: Calories: 472, Protein: 3 gm., Carbohydrates: 55 gm., Fat: 26 gm.

Mustard or Collard Greens

2 bunches greens or 1 if the bunches are large
½ onion, thinly sliced
1 tablespoon oil
½ teaspoon salt
⅛ teaspoon cayenne
½ to 1 cup water (if the greens are tough)

Wash each leaf of the greens, and take out the large stalk in the center. Break them, or cut with scissors, into small pieces, and set aside. Sauté the onion in the oil until it begins to turn brown. This gives a good flavor to the greens. Add the greens, salt, and cayenne, and simmer on low heat until tender, stirring often. I don't use water for most greens. If you can easily eat them raw, they need very little cooking and no water. Collard greens may need a little longer cooking time and sometimes a little water, especially if they are older greens.

Serves 4 to 6

Per serving: Calories: 87, Protein: 3 gm.,
Carbohydrates: 11 gm., Fat: 3 gm.

Turnips and Greens

2 bunches turnips and their
  greens
1 tablespoon oil
1 medium onion, thinly
  sliced
½ teaspoon salt
⅛ teaspoon cayenne
½ cup water

Wash the greens and turnips. Dice the turnips and cut the greens up into small pieces. Sauté the turnips in the oil for 10 minutes, stirring often. Add the onion and simmer, stirring often, until the onions and the turnips begin to brown a little. Add the remaining ingredients and simmer until the turnips and greens are tender, about 20 minutes. More water may be added for tougher greens. They may also need a little more time to cook.

Serves 4 to 6

*Per serving: Calories: 68, Protein: 1 gm.,
Carbohydrates: 10 gm., Fat: 3 gm.*

Mashed Potatoes

4 large potatoes, cubed
2 tablespoons oil
½ teaspoon salt
½ cup water or low-fat
  soymilk

Steam the potatoes until tender. Place in a bowl and add the remaining ingredients. Mash well with a potato masher. This should be done right before serving. More soymilk may be added for a creamier mashed potato. These are delicious served with Brown Gravy (page 13).

Serves 4

*Per serving: Calories: 244, Protein: 3 gm.,
Carbohydrates: 41 gm., Fat: 7 gm.*

New Potatoes and Green Beans

12 small red potatoes
1 lb green beans
½ red onion, thinly sliced
2 tablespoons oil
½ teaspoon salt

My grandmother used to call little red potatoes "new potatoes." Maybe because when they were little they were new. Hence the name New Potatoes and Green Beans.

Steam the potatoes and green beans separately until tender, and set aside. Sauté the onion in the oil for 5 minutes, add the potatoes, green beans, and salt, and sauté for another 15 minutes.

Serves 4

Per serving: Calories: 247, Protein: 4 gm., Carbohydrates: 43 gm., Fat: 7 gm.

Parsley Potatoes

4 medium potatoes, diced or
   12 small whole red
   potatoes
2 tablespoons oil
1 cup fresh parsley minced
½ teaspoon salt
⅛ teaspoon cayenne

This was one of MaMa's favorite ways to fix red potatoes.

Steam the potatoes until tender, and sauté in the oil for 10 minutes. Add the parsley, salt, and cayenne, and simmer for an additional 10 minutes.

Serves 4

Per serving: Calories: 239, Protein: 3 gm., Carbohydrates: 42 gm., Fat: 7 gm.

Potato Fritters

¾ cup chick-pea flour
  (garbanzo flour)
¼ cup corn flour
¼ cup nutritional yeast flakes
¼ cup whole wheat pastry
  flour
½ teaspoon salt
¼ teaspoon paprika
¼ teaspoon cayenne
1 cup water
4 medium potatoes, shredded
1 small onion, minced
oil for frying

Mix all of the ingredients together, except the potatoes, onion, and oil. The mix should resemble a thick pancake batter. More water may be added if it is too thick, or more chick-pea flour may be added if it is too thin. Add the potatoes and onion, and drop by spoon fulls into ½ inch hot oil. Fry on each side until golden. Place on a piece of paper bag to drain the oil.

Serves 4 to 6

*Per serving: Calories: 335, Protein: 8 gm.,
Carbohydrates: 49 gm., Fat: 12 gm.*

Hazel's Fried Corn

∎∎

12 ears fresh corn
3 tablespoons oil
½ teaspoon salt

This is one of my favorite recipe's that my mother-in-law makes. She's from Mississippi and their cooking was a little different than my grandmother's but just as delicious. She always makes this for us when we go home.

Fresh corn is best but frozen may be used. For fresh corn, slice the top half off of each kernel. Scrape the corn remaining on the cob with a knife, directly into a 12-inch, black skillet. This makes it really rich. Place the corn in the skillet with the oil and salt, and fry until it starts to brown. Flip often with a spatula, and scrape the bottom of the skillet. This gets all of the brown crust off the bottom of the skillet which is really delicious when mixed with the corn.

Serves 4

Per serving: Calories: 247, Protein: 4 gm., Carbohydrates: 43 gm., Fat: 7 gm.

Scalloped Eggplant

■ ■

1 large eggplant, diced
2 cups mushrooms, thinly
 sliced
1 onion, thinly sliced
1 bell pepper, thinly sliced
3 tablespoons oil
1 cup low-fat soymilk
2 cups toasted bread crumbs
1 teaspoon salt
½ teaspoon paprika
⅛ teaspoon cayenne
1 cup Yeast Cheese Sauce
 (page 84) or 1 cup soy
 mozzarella cheese,
 shredded

Preheat the oven to 350°. In a large skillet, sauté the eggplant, mushrooms, onion, and bell pepper in the oil until the eggplant becomes tender, about 10 to 15 minutes. Add the soymilk, 1 cup of bread crumbs, and the spices, and stir well. Place in a baking dish, and top with the remaining bread crumbs and the Yeast Cheese Sauce. Bake for 25 minutes.

Serves 4 to 6

Per serving: Calories: 339, Protein: 10 gm., Carbohydrates: 49 gm., Fat: 9 gm.

Macaroni and Cheese

½ onion, minced
2 teaspoons oil
2 lbs soy macaroni
12 cups water
1 tablespoon oil
½ teaspoon salt
2 cups Yeast Cheese Sauce
  (page 84)
½ cup soymilk
½ teaspoon salt
¼ teaspoon paprika
⅛ teaspoon cayenne

In a skillet, sauté the onion in 2 teaspoons of oil for 10 minutes, and set aside. Add the macaroni to boiling water along with 1 tablespoon of oil and ½ teaspoon of salt. Cook the macaroni until tender, drain, and rinse with hot water. Preheat the oven to 350°. Mix the onion and noodles. Combine the Yeast Cheese Sauce, soymilk, and spices in a blender to make a thick, creamy sauce. Pour over the macaroni and stir. Place in an 8 x 8-inch baking dish, and bake for 25 minutes.

Serves 4 to 6

*Per serving: Calories: 339, Protein: 16 gm.,
Carbohydrates: 57 gm., Fat: 4 gm.*

Smothered Cabbage

1 small onion, minced
2 tablespoons oil
1 medium cabbage, cut into
  2-inch squares
3 cloves garlic, finely
  shredded
½ teaspoon salt
¼ teaspoon paprika
⅛ teaspoon cayenne
½ cup water

This dish is better if it is not over cooked. Sauté the onion in the oil for 10 minutes, and add the cabbage and garlic. Sauté for an additional 10 minutes, stirring often. Add the remaining ingredients, and simmer for 15 minutes or until tender.

Serves 4

*Per serving: Calories: 74, Protein: 2 gm.,
Carbohydrates: 9 gm., Fat: 3 gm.*

Yeast Cheese Sauce

1 cup nutritional yeast flakes
¼ cup whole wheat pastry
  flour
2 tablespoons arrowroot
  powder
1 teaspoon salt
2 cups water
2 teaspoons oil
2 teaspoons mustard

Mix the dry ingredients and whisk in the water. Mix well to remove lumps. Cook in a double boiler, stirring often, until it begins to thicken. Remove from the heat and stir in the oil and mustard. The sauce will thicken as it cools. More water may be added to make a thinner sauce.

Makes 3 cups

Per ¼ cup: Calories: 55, Protein: 4 gm., Carbohydrates: 7 gm., Fat: 1 gm.

Pecan Mushroom Sauce

2 cups mushrooms, thinly
  sliced
2 tablespoons oil
1 onion, minced
3 tablespoons almond butter
2 tablespoons tamari
½ cup pecans, chopped
1½ cups water
¼ teaspoon salt
⅛ teaspoon cayenne
  (optional)

Sauté the mushrooms in the oil until they begin to brown. Add the onion and cook until it becomes translucent. Add the remaining ingredients, and cook on low heat until the sauce thickens. You can add more water to make a thinner sauce. Serve over potatoes, sliced toast, or gluten.

Makes 4 cups

Per ¼ cup: Calories: 64, Protein: 1 gm., Carbohydrates: 3 gm., Fat: 4 gm.

Southern Tomato Sauce

1 medium onion, minced
2 small bell peppers, thinly
  sliced
2 teaspoons oil
3 stalks celery, minced
6 cloves garlic, finely
  shredded
12 medium tomatoes, diced
1½ teaspoons salt
½ teaspoon thyme
1 teaspoon basil
1 tablespoon paprika
⅛ teaspoon cayenne

Sauté the onion and bell peppers in the oil for 10 minutes, stirring often. Add the remaining ingredients and cook on low heat for 1 hour, stirring frequently. Serve over rice or noodles.

Makes approximately 4 cups

Per cup: Calories: 119, Protein: 3 gm., Carbohydrates: 20 gm., Fat: 2 gm.

Cranberry Sauce

2 cups cranberries
½ cup honey
1 tablespoon arrowroot
1 tablespoon water

Steam the cranberries until they become tender, about 20 minutes, and set aside. In a separate pot, cook the honey on low heat for 15 minutes, stirring often. Add the cranberries and simmer for 10 minutes. Mix the arrowroot and water until all of the lumps are dissolved, and add to the cranberries and honey. Simmer until it becomes thick, stirring constantly, about 5 minutes.

Makes 2½ cups

Per ¼ cup: Calories: 62, Protein: 0 gm., Carbohydrates: 15 gm., Fat: 0 gm.

Breads

Basic Whole Wheat Bread

■■

2 tablespoons active dry yeast
2 tablespoons oil
5 tablespoons honey
2 cups warm water
7 cups whole wheat pastry
  flour
2 teaspoons salt

In a large bowl, mix the yeast, oil, 3 tablespoons of the honey, and 1 cup of the warm water. Let this set for 10 minutes or until the yeast begins to foam a little. Stir twice and add the remaining honey and warm water. In a separate bowl, mix the flour and salt, add to the yeast mixture, and knead for 15 minutes or until you have a smooth dough. Set the dough aside in an oiled bowl, cover with a damp dish towel, and let rise in a warm place until double in size. Break it into two parts, form into loaves, and place in two oiled and lightly floured bread pans. Again, cover with a damp kitchen towel, and let rise until double. Bake at 350° for 45 minutes.

Makes 2 loaves

Per slice (8 slices per loaf): Calories: 213, Protein: 7 gm., Carbohydrates: 40 gm., Fat: 2 gm.

Variations ☛ *By using the basic whole wheat bread recipe, you can create any kind of nut or dried veggie bread you like. Here are a few examples of some of my favorites.*

☛ ## Pecan Bread

When making the Basic Whole Wheat Bread (page 87), simply add **1½ cups chopped pecans** to the recipe when adding the salt and flour. Walnuts or pecans are my favorite, but you can use any nut you like.

Makes 2 loaves

Per slice (8 slices per loaf): Calories: 285, Protein: 8 gm., Carbohydrates: 42 gm., Fat: 6 gm.

☛ Tomato Bread

Soak **1½ cups chopped, dried tomatoes** in hot water until soft, and drain. Follow the directions for Basic Whole Wheat Bread (page 87), and add the tomatoes at the same time you add the remaining water and honey to the yeast mixture.

Makes 2 loaves

Per slice (8 slices per loaf): Calories: 222, Protein: 7 gm., Carbohydrates: 42 gm., Fat: 2 gm.

☛ Onion Bread

When making Basic Whole Wheat Bread (page 87), add **1½ cups chopped, sautéed onions** when you add the remaining water and honey to the yeast mixture.

Makes 2 loaves

Per slice (8 slices per loaf): Calories: 221, Protein: 7 gm., Carbohydrates: 41 gm., Fat: 2 gm.

Herb Rolls

2 tablespoons basil
2 teaspoons rosemary
1 teaspoon oregano

Use the Basic Whole Wheat Bread recipe (page 87), and add the spices at the same time the salt and flour are mixed together. When dividing the dough, instead of making two loaves, simply form into rolls approximately 3 inches wide by 2 inches thick, and place side by side in a rectangle baking pan. Cover with a damp cloth, and let rise the same as you would the loaves. Bake at 350° for 45 minutes.

Makes approximately 20 rolls

Per roll: Calories: 171, Protein: 6 gm.,
Carbohydrates: 32 gm., Fat: 2 gm.

French Bread

Use the Basic Whole Wheat Bread recipe (page 87), divide the dough into two parts, and make two long thin loaves. Place the loves on an oiled cookie sheet, and make three slices across the top of each loaf with a sharp knife. Cover with a damp cloth, and let rise until double in size. When baking, place a pot of boiling water in the bottom of the oven. Bake at 350° for 45 minutes. Ten minutes before the bread is done, brush the tops with oil.

Makes 2 loaves

Per slice (8 slices per loaf): Calories: 213, Protein: 7 gm.,
Carbohydrates: 40 gm., Fat: 2 gm.

Corn Bread

■ ■

¾ cup corn meal or corn
 flour
1 cup whole wheat pastry
 flour
3 teaspoons baking powder
1 teaspoon salt
¼ cup oil
1 cup water, or low-fat
 soymilk

Mix all of the ingredients, and place in a hot, oiled skillet. Bake at 350° for 25 to 30 minutes or until golden.

Serves 4 to 6

Per serving: Calories: 251, Protein: 5 gm., Carbohydrates: 32 gm., Fat: 12 gm.

Variations ☛ ### Jalapeño Corn Bread

Add to the Corn Bread recipe **2 to 3 tablespoons shredded jalapeño**, depending on how hot you like it.

Serves 4 to 6

Per serving: Calories: 252, Protein: 5 gm., Carbohydrates: 32 gm., Fat: 12 gm.

☛ ### Onion Corn Bread

Add to the Corn Bread recipe **½ cup sautéed chopped onions.**

Serves 4 to 6

Per serving: Calories: 264, Protein: 5 gm., Carbohydrates: 33 gm., Fat: 12 gm.

Hush Puppies

1½ cups corn meal or corn
   flour
1½ cups water
⅓ cup soymilk
1 tablespoon oil
1 small onion, minced
2 cloves garlic, minced
¼ cup green onion, minced
1 cup whole wheat pastry
   flour
3 teaspoons baking powder
2½ teaspoons salt
¼ teaspoon cayenne
   oil for frying

In a skillet, mix the corn meal and water, and cook until the corn meal begins to roll into a ball. Set aside. Mix all of the remaining ingredients, and add to the corn meal. Take 2 to 3 tablespoons of the mixture, form into a ball, and deep fry in 2 inches of hot oil. The balls can also be baked. Place the balls on an oiled cookie sheet, brush with oil, and bake at 375° for 25 minutes or until golden. Delicious served with any kind of cooked beans and greens.

Makes approximately 16 hush puppies

Per hush puppie (deep fried): Calories: 112, Protein: 2 gm., Carbohydrates: 15 gm., Fat: 4 gm.

Per hush puppie (baked): Calories: 90, Protein: 2 gm., Carbohydrates: 15 gm., Fat: 2 gm.

Desserts

Whole Wheat Pie Crust

3 cups whole wheat pastry flour
1¼ teaspoons salt
¾ cup soy margarine
⅓ cup plus 2 tablespoons ice water

Mix the flour and salt, and add the margarine and water a little at a time until the dough becomes smooth and easy to handle. I usually use my hands to mix it well. Divide the dough into two parts. Place on a floured counter top or cutting board, sprinkle the top of the dough with a little flour, and roll out with a rolling pin or jar. You can also roll the dough out between two pieces of waxed paper. Roll each portion out into a 10 inch circle, and place in a pie pan. Punch holes in the bottom of the pie shell with a fork before baking to keep it from bubbling up.

Makes 2 crusts (8 servings each)

Per serving: Calories: 151, Protein: 3 gm., Carbohydrates: 15 gm., Fat: 8 gm.

Apple or Peach Pie

■■

4 large tart apples or peaches,
   thinly sliced
¾ cup honey
2 teaspoons cinnamon
⅓ cup arrowroot
⅓ cup water
Whole Wheat Pie Crust
   (page 93)

Place the sliced apples or peaches, honey, and cinnamon in a saucepan on medium heat until the apples begin to wilt, stirring often. In a separate bowl, mix the arrowroot and water until all of the lumps are dissolved. Add to the apple mixture, and stir well while simmering for 2 or 3 minutes. Preheat the oven to 350°. Pour the apple mixture into two pie shells, and cover the tops of the pies with ¼ inch strips of pie dough, making a crisscross pattern. Pinch the edges of the pie dough with your fingers to make a decorative finish, and cut off the excess dough with a knife. Bake for 30 minutes or until golden brown. For a pretty finish, brush honey and cinnamon over the top.

Makes 2 pies (8 servings each)

Per serving: Calories: 249, Protein: 3 gm., Carbohydrates: 39 gm., Fat: 8 gm.

Pumpkin Pie

■■■

4 cups pumpkin, steamed and
  mashed
⅔ cup soymilk
½ cup arrowroot powder
4 tablespoons creamy peanut
  butter
¾ cups honey
2 tablespoons cinnamon
½ teaspoon vanilla
¾ teaspoon salt
Wole Wheat Pie Crust
  (page 93)

Preheat the oven to 400°. Combine all of the ingredients with a wire whisk, blender, or food processor until everything is well mixed. Pour into a pie shell, and bake for 20 minutes. Lower the heat to 275°, and bake for an additional 45 minutes. Let cool and serve.

Makes 2 small pies or 1 thick large pie (serves 16)

Per serving: Calories: 261, Protein: 4 gm., Carbohydrates: 36 gm., Fat: 10 gm.

Variation ☛ **Yam Pie**

Same as Pumpkin Pie but use **yams** instead of pumpkin, and add **3 tablespoons molasses**.

Makes 2 small pies or 1 thick large pie (serves 16)

Per serving: Calories: 288, Protein: 4 gm., Carbohydrates: 43 gm., Fat: 10 gm.

Tasty Tarts

■■■■■■■■■■■■■■■■■■■■■■■■■■■■■■■■■■■■■■ ■■

The regular Whole Wheat Crust recipe (page 93) may be used to make tarts instead of regular pies. To do this, roll the dough out as you usually would, and use a saucer to cut the dough into circles. Preheat the oven to 350°. Place ⅓ cup of pie filling in the center, fold over, and seal the edges with a fork. Make three ½-inch slits in the top of each tart to let the steam out while baking. Bake for 30 minutes or until golden. Tarts can be made in different shapes such as triangles or rectangles.

Makes 8 small tarts

Bread Pudding

■ ■

3½ cups soymilk
1 tablespoon vanilla
½ cup honey
¼ teaspoon salt
8 cups stale French bread
   sliced ¼ inch thick
   (regular bread may be
   used)
3 tablespoons oil

This was another way my grandmother used stale French bread. After our trips to and from Louisiana , or after visits from our relatives, who always brought a lot of bakery goods, we had an abundance of French bread.

Preheat the oven to 325°. Combine the milk, vanilla, honey, and salt for 3 minutes in the blender, or beat with a wire whisk, until all of the ingredients are well mixed. Place in a large enough bowl to hold the bread. Stir in the bread making sure that all the slices of bread are thoroughly covered with the liquid. Place in a rectangle baking pan, dribble the oil over the top, and bake for 25 minutes or until the top begins to brown.

Serves 6 to 8

Per serving: Calories: 245, Protein: 6 gm., Carbohydrates: 35 gm., Fat: 9 gm.

Banana Bread

■ ■

2 cups whole wheat pastry
   flour
¼ teaspoon salt
1 tablespoon baking powder
½ cup walnuts or pecans,
   chopped
¼ cup oil
¾ cup honey
½ cup soymilk or water
1 cup bananas, mashed
1 teaspoon vanilla

Preheat the oven to 350°. Mix the dry ingredients together. In a separate bowl, mix the wet ingredients. Combine the two mixtures and stir well. Bake in small loaf pans or in a cake pan. Oil the pans and sprinkle with a little flour to prevent sticking. Bake for 45 minutes. This recipe may take up to an hour to bake, depending on how thick you make it. You can check it by sticking a toothpick in the middle. If it comes out dry, it's done.

Makes 12 slices

Per slice: Calories: 224, Protein: 4 gm.,
Carbohydrates: 34 gm., Fat: 7 gm.

Variation ☛

Fruit Bread
Made the same as Banana Bread, but use **1 cup frozen cherries or 1 cup peaches, thinly sliced or 1 cup pears, thinly sliced** in place of the bananas.

Simón's Lemon Bars

Crust:
**2 cups whole wheat pastry
  flour**
½ cup honey
½ cup soy margarine
2 teaspoons baking powder
½ teaspoon salt

Filling:
1 cup honey
**½ cup finely shredded
  lemon peel**
½ cup lemon juice
¼ teaspoon salt
4 tablespoons arrowroot
3 tablespoons water
½ cup coconut powder

Preheat the oven to 325°. To make the crust, mix the flour, margarine, baking powder, and salt. Roll out ¼ inch thick, and bake in a 8-inch square baking pan until golden, about 20 minutes.

To make the filling, mix the honey, lemon peel, lemon juice, and salt in a saucepan, and cook for 10 minutes on medium high heat. In a separate bowl, mix the arrowroot and water. Stir into the honey mixture, and cook for an additional 10 minutes on medium heat, stirring constantly. Place the filling on the crust, sprinkle the top with the coconut, cool, and serve.

Makes 16 pieces

*Per piece: Calories: 254, Protein: 2 gm.,
Carbohydrates: 38 gm., Fat: 10 gm.*

Basic Vanilla Cake

1 teaspoon salt
⅔ cup oil
1½ cups honey
¾ to 1 cup soymilk
4 teaspoons vanilla
4 cups whole wheat pastry
   flour
4 teaspoons baking powder

Preheat the oven to 350°. Mix all of the wet ingredients together well. In a separate bowl, mix all of the dry ingredients together. Combine the two and mix well. Divide into two oiled and flour 8-inch cake pans, and bake for 30 minutes or until golden. Let cool and spread with your favorite icing.

Makes 16 slices

Per slice: Calories: 277, Protein: 4 gm., Carbohydrates: 44 gm., Fat: 9 gm.

Variations ☛ **Carob Cake**

Made the same as Vanilla Cake, but instead of the 4 cups of flour, add **3 cups whole wheat pastry flour** and **1 cup carob powder**.

Makes 16 slices

Per slice: Calories: 266, Protein: 3 gm., Carbohydrates: 42 gm., Fat: 9 gm.

☞ Lemon Cake

Made the same as Vanilla Cake, but instead of the vanilla, add **¼ cup lemon juice** and **2 tablespoons shredded lemon rind.**

Makes 16 slices

Per slice: Calories: 283, Protein: 4 gm., Carbohydrates: 45 gm., Fat: 9 gm.

☞ Coconut Cake

Made the same as the Vanilla Cake, but add **¾ cup shredded coconut** that has been soaked in hot water for 20 minutes and drained well.

Makes 16 slices

Per slice: Calories: 354, Protein: 5 gm., Carbohydrates: 47 gm., Fat: 16 gm.

Carrot Cake

4 cups whole wheat pastry
  flour
4 teaspoons baking powder
1 teaspoon salt
2 teaspoons cinnamon
½ teaspoon allspice
¾ cup oil
1½ cups honey
3 cups shredded carrots
1½ cups walnuts chopped
½ cup raisins

Preheat the oven to 350°. Mix all of the wet ingredients together well. In a separate bowl, mix all of the dry ingredients. Combine the two and mix well. Bake in a 9 x 13-inch pan for 45 minutes or until golden. This cake is good with Spice Icing (page 103).

Makes 16 slices

Per serving: Calories: 382, Protein: 5 gm., Carbohydrates: 51 gm., Fat: 16 gm.

Vanilla Icing

1 cup soy margarine
1 cup soy powder or rice
  polish
¾ to 1 cup honey
1 teaspoon vanilla

Mix all of the ingredients with a mixer until creamy smooth. If it seems too dry, add a little soymilk 1 tablespoon at a time until it is creamy but thick.

Per piece of cake (1/16): Calories: 127, Protein: 3 gm., Carbohydrates: 16 gm., Fat: 6 gm.

Variations ☞ **Carob Icing**

Made the same as Vanilla Icing, but instead of 1 cup soy powder, use **½ cup soy flour** or **rice polish** and **½ cup toasted or raw carob powder.**

Per piece of cake (1/16): Calories: 130, Protein: 1 gm., Carbohydrates: 18 gm., Fat: 6 gm.

☞ **Coconut Icing**

Made the same as Vanilla Icing and add **½ cup shredded coconut.**

Per piece of cake (1/16): Calories: 174, Protein: 3 gm., Carbohydrates: 17 gm., Fat: 10 gm.

☞ **Lemon Icing**

Made the same as Vanilla Icing, but instead of vanilla, add **2 tablespoons lemon juice,** and **1 tablespoon shredded lemon rind.**

Per piece of cake (1/16): Calories: 127, Protein: 3 gm., Carbohydrates: 16 gm., Fat: 6 gm.

☞ **Spice Icing**

Made the same as Vanilla Icing, and add **1½ teaspoons cinnamon, ¼ teaspoon cloves,** and **⅛ teaspoon allspice.**

Per piece of cake (1/16): Calories: 127, Protein: 3 gm., Carbohydrates: 16 gm., Fat: 6 gm.

Index

A

Apple or Peach Pie   94
Avocado Salad   25

B

Banana Bread   98
Barbecue Gluten   47
Bars, Simón's Lemon   99
Basic Vanilla Cake   100
Basic Whole Wheat Bread   87
Bayou Teche Candied Yams   72
BBQ Sandwich   42
Biscuits
   and Cream Gravy   12
   Onion   12
Black-Eyed Peas, Broussard   70
Blackened Tofu   64
Boulettes
   Sweet   68
   Vegetable   67
Bread
   Banana   98
   Basic Whole Wheat   87
   Corn   90
   French   89
   Onion   88
   Pudding   97
   Tomato   88
Breaded Tofu   14
Broussard Black-Eyed Peas   70

C

Cabbage
   Dupois', Rolls   53
Cajun
   Dip   55
   Meatless Patties   56
   Seasoning   55
   Tofu or Eggplant   48
Cake
   Basic Vanilla   100
   Carob   100
   Carrot   102
   Coconut   101
   Lemon   101
Candied Yams, Bayou Teche   72
Carob
   Cake   100
   Icing   103
Carrot
   Cake   102
   Raisin Salad   25
Cauliflower Au Gratin   73
Chicory Coffee   17
Chili, Taunt Malute's   31
Chowder, Corn   34
Coconut
   Cake   101
   Icing   103
Coffee, Chicory   17
Cole Slaw, MaMa's   26
Corn
   Chowder   34
   Hazel's Fried   81
Corn Bread   90
Cornbread Dressing   50
Courtboullion, Creole   57
Coush Coush   16
Cranberry Sauce   85

Creole
    Courtboullion   57
    Gluten   46
Cucumber Salad   26

D

Darkened Tofu   21
Dip, Cajun   55
Dirty Rice   52
Donna's Vinaigrette Dressing   29
Dressing
    Donna's Vinaigrette   29
    French   29
Dressing (stuffing)
    Cornbread   50
    Eggplant   62
    Pecan Rice   51
    Pepper   61
Dry Roux   37
Dumplings, Vegetable Stew and   49
Dupois' Cabbage Rolls   53
Dwayne's Julienne French Fries   76

E

Eggplant
    Cajun or Tofu   48
    Dressing   62
    Scalloped   82
Etoufee, Vegetable   66

F

fat, reducing the amount of   5
French
    Bread   89
    Dressing   29
    Dwayne's Julienne, Fries   76
    Fried Onion Rings   74
    Potato Salad   27

Fried
    Grits   16
    Veggie Platter   54
Fruit
    Over Toast   20
    Preserves   22

G

Gluten   45
    Barbecue   47
    Creole   46
Gravy
    Brown   13
    Brown Mushroom   13
    Cream   12
Greens
    Mustard or Collard   77
    Turnips and   78
Grits   15
Grits, Fried   16
Gumbo   36
Gumbo Des Herbes   39
Gumbo With a Dry Roux   38

H

Hazel's Fried Corn   81
Herb Rolls   89
Homefried Scramble   11
Hush Puppies   91

I

Icing
    Carob   103
    Coconut   103
    Lemon   103
    Spice   103
    Vanilla   102
Introduction   5

J

Jambalaya   58

L

Lafayette Lima Beans   71
Lemon
  Cake   101
  Icing   103
Lima Bean
  Soup   34
Lima Beans
  Lafayette   71
Louisiana Spaghetti   60

M

Macaroni and Cheese   83
Mail Order Companies   9
MaMa's Cole Slaw   26
Mashed Potatoes   78
Mixed Greens Salad   27
Mustard or Collard Greens   77

N

Navy Bean Soup   32
New Potatoes and Green Beans   79
Not Pigs in a Blanket   18
Notes From Our Kitchen   6

O

Onion
  Bread   88
  French Fried, Rings   74

P

Pan Perdue   17
Pancakes   18

Parsley Potatoes   79
Pear Preserves   22
Pecan
  Mushroom Sauce   84
  Rice Dressing   51
Pepper Dressing   61
Peppered Tofu   20
Pie
  Apple or Peach   94
  Pumpkin   95
Pie Crust, Whole Wheat   93
Po Boys   40
Potato
  Fritters   80
  Soup   33
  Stew   59
Potatoes
  Mashed   78
  New, and Green Beans   79
  Parsley   79
  Southern   75
Preserves
  Fruit   22
  Pear   22
  Watermelon Rind   23
Pudding, Bread   97
Pumpkin Pie   95

R

Red Beans and Rice   63
Rice
  Burger Patties   43
  Dirty   52
  Pecan, Dressing   51
  Red Beans and   63
  Smothered Okra Over   64
Rolls, Herb   89
Roux, Dry   37

S

Salad
  Avocado   25
  Cucumber   26
  French Potato   27
  Mixed Greens   27
  Sweet Pea   28
  Tofu   28
Sandwiches
  BBQ   42
  Po Boys   40
  Rice Burger Patties   43
  Sloppy Joe's   41
Sauce
  Cranberry   85
  Pecan Mushroom   84
  Southern Tomato   85
  Yeast Cheese   84
Saucisse   19
Scalloped Eggplant   82
Scrambled Tofu   21
Simón's Lemon Bars   99
Sloppy Joe's   41
Smothered Okra Over Rice   64
Soup
  Corn Chowder   34
  Gumbo   36
  Gumbo Des Herbes   39
  Gumbo With a Dry Roux   38
  Lima Bean   34
  Navy Bean   32
  Potato   33
  Vegetable   35
Southern
  Homefries   11
  Potatoes   75
  Tomato Sauce   85
Spaghetti, Louisiana   60

Spice Icing   103
Stew
  Potato   59
  Vegetable, and Dumplings   49
Stuffed Peppers   65
Sweet Boulettes   68
Sweet Pea Salad   28

T

Tasty Tarts   96
Taunt Malute's Chili   31
Tofu
  Breaded   14
  Cajun, or Eggplant   48
  Darkened   21
  Peppered   20
  Salad   28
  Scrambled   21
Tomato Bread   88
Turnips and Greens   78

V

Vanilla Icing   102
Vegetable
  Boulettes   67
  Etoufee   66
  Soup   35
  Stew and Dumplings   49

W

Watermelon Rind Preserves   23
Whole Wheat Pie Crust   93

Y

Yeast Cheese Sauce   84

Other fine cookbooks from
THE BOOK PUBLISHING COMPANY

Almost-No Fat Cookbook $10.95

American Harvest 11.95

Burgers 'n Fries 'n Cinnamon Buns 6.95

Cookin' Healthy with One Foot Out the Door 8.95

Cooking with Gluten and Seitan 7.95

Ecological Cooking: Recipes to Save the Planet 10.95

Fabulous Beans 9.95

From A Traditional Greek Kitchen 9.95

Good Time Eatin' in Cajun Country 9.95

George Bernard Shaw Vegetarian Cookbook 8.95

Healthy Cook's Kitchen Companion 12.95

Holiday Diet Book 9.95

Instead of Chicken, Instead of Turkey 9.95

Judy Brown's Guide to Natural Foods Cooking 10.95

Kids Can Cook 9.95

Murrieta Hot Springs Vegetarian Cookbook 9.95

New Farm Vegetarian Cookbook 8.95

Now & Zen Epicure 17.95

Olive Oil Cookery 11.95

Peaceful Cook 8.95

Physician's Slimming Guide, Neal D. Barnard, M.D. 5.95
    Also by Dr. Barnard:
    Foods That Cause You To Lose Weight 12.95
    Live Longer, Live Better (90 min. cassette) 9.95
    Beyond Animal Experiments (90 min. cassette) 9.95

Shiitake Way $7.95
Shoshoni Cookbook 12.95
Simply Heavenly 19.95
Soups For All Seasons 9.95
The Sprout Garden 8.95
Starting Over: Learning to Cook with Natural Foods 10.95
Tempeh Cookbook 10.95
Ten Talents (Vegetarian Cookbook) 18.95
Tofu Cookery 14.95
Tofu Quick & Easy 7.95
TVP Cookbook 6.95
Uncheese Cookbook 11.95
Uprisings: The Whole Grain Bakers' Book 13.95
Vegetarian Cooking for People with Diabetes 10.95

Ask your store to carry these books, or you may order directly from:
The Book Publishing Company
P.O. Box 99
Summertown, TN 38483
Or call: 1-800-695-2241
Please add $2.50 per book for shipping